DASH DIET

COOKBOOK

365 DAYS OF HEART-HEALTHY RECIPES TO LOWER YOUR BLOOD PRESSURE & LOSE WEIGHT

D1706338

BY DEBBY HAYES

TABLE OF CONTENTS

INTRODUCTION

The DASH Diet (Dietary Approaches to Stop Hypertension) is a diet that was created by the National Institute of Health's National Heart, Lung, and Blood Institute in 1993. The diet was designed to help those people already suffering from or at risk of developing hypertension (high blood pressure).

The ultimate risk with consistently high blood pressure (hypertension) is that it can eventually place enough pressure on artery walls to cause damage and blockage, leading to a heart attack, stroke, and heart disease.

Scientists have determined that your diet helps prevent hypertension and can also help reverse it as well.

Today, experts still rank the DASH diet #1 for preventing and reversing heart disease. In fact, the DASH diet has proven to lower blood pressure within two weeks; it is so swift-acting.

The Benefits of the DASH DIET

A recent study published June 1, 2021, found that a reduced-sodium DASH diet can help reduce blood pressure and improve markers for cardiovascular health due to heart attack or stroke.

The DASH diet's many benefits are now well known. It has proven to lower blood pressure in 14 days, lower the incidence of heart attack and stroke and lower LDL (bad) cholesterol - the two major risk factors for stroke and heart disease.

People who follow the DASH diet are also far less likely to develop diabetes than those who follow a regular diet. In recent studies, the DASH diet proved to enhance cognitive function as well as prevent the onset of dementia in the elderly.

In 2021, for the 23rd year in a row, the DASH diet remains in the top position for those individuals seeking to improve health and avoid a long list of chronic diseases like obesity, diabetes, metabolic syndrome, and cardiovascular disease.

Because of this, the DASH diet is key in helping people live longer, healthier, more joyful lives.

My Story: From Obese to Obeser? And I'm On a Diet!?

My story is like so many other women's stories of weight gain, weight loss, weight gain, then finally coming to accept myself as obese – only to discover my health was now in danger, and there was no time to "accept myself" as anything but in a state of serious and immediate danger.

I have two children, four and six years old. I wouldn't trade having them for anything. However, pregnancy does cause weight gain, and my weight suddenly skyrocketed past 200 lbs. and I stayed there (at five ft. four inches!) with my second child.

First, I tried the ketogenic diet. Although I lost some initial weight, I felt so debilitated and drained to a point where I couldn't get up off the couch and take care of two kids. I needed more carbohydrates – I needed my big salads, grilled veggies, and my beloved grainy-seedy bread sandwiches.

What I've found with restrictive diets of any kind is that my body becomes so hungry for whatever is denied it, and I must go replenish and eat that thing that was denied.

But after a long period of deprivation, I'm so hungry for – say, sandwiches, that I tend to eat until I finally hit some meter that says "satisfied". Usually, this takes me not only back up to my original weight before the diet – but makes me gain weight well past my original mark.

I now firmly believe deprivation diets don't work for a long list of reasons. But chiefly – and this is important – because they are STRESS. Stress causes cortisol release, which produces belly fat. No wonder deprivation diets always result in failure, right?!

That's why I think the DASH diet works. It's not about any kind of deprivation.

At all.

But back to my story, and here comes the frightening part...

So, I replenished my carbs and nutrients until I felt I could get off the couch and found my derriere had become a pendulous weight that could not be moved without major effort. I was mad. It wasn't as if I'd been sitting around eating bon bons.

I was simply trying to recapture energy denied me from a measly 5% allotment for healthful foods like veggies, fruits, and grains that I was sorely deprived of on keto.

Obviously, something was not right about this diet for me, even though the payoffs were supposed to be so grand and worth it.

But I figured I just wasn't staying in ketosis–and tried harder.

Soon, I was developing rheumatoid osteoarthritis in my feet from carrying excess weight. I was 38 and walking with a cane. I was on various medications, including one for fibromyalgia.

This particular medication caused me to gain a whopping 1 pound a day. And I had no vitamins and minerals coming in because I was on a diet of 80% fat.

I soon abandoned the keto diet, ate a crazy amount of fast food and pastries I had been denied so long, and I soon weighed a frightening 240 lbs.

I avoided mirrors. My face was lost in a sea of flesh.

I lost all self-esteem. My husband left me, and I sank into a deep depression.

Enter: The Life-Saving, Craving Crushing DASH diet

I started attending OA meetings, as recommended by my very fed-up doctor. I was hoping they might help me curb the fast food and frozen cheesecake-eating problem that followed my ketogenic fiasco diet.

And I met some of the smartest, most down to earth women I had ever met in my life. Ultimately they became some of my best friends.

Like my doctor, they were as convinced of the wonders of the DASH diet as he was.

I thought OA would be a lot of stories of failure in the face of food. But I heard story after story of triumph.

I learned how the DASH diet not only helped men and women lose weight but how it had helped them utterly reverse pre-diabetes diagnoses and lower blood pressure and cholesterol in time to reverse risks of heart disease, heart attack, and stroke.

Most of all, they had been released from the deadly prison of restrictive diets and enabled them to live life fully, eating as a normal person would–but get healthy and lose weight at the same time.

So I asked the group, "I guess you guys are going to have to change the name to HEA – Healthy Eaters Anonymous?"

I was still hedging, and I was not quite ready to give up a new addiction – Sonic. A double cheeseburger with extra ketchup, pickles and onions with one of those kiwi-lime-cherry drinks and I was a happy girl.

But a visit to the doctor in 2018 sealed the deal...

"It is time for action, not debate," he said grimly.

"It is exactly as I feared." He looked at me very concerned over his glasses, adding,

"Your A1C is at 5.9%, which indicates pre-diabetes. You also have the markers for pre-hypertension. It's time for change – right now. This is now a life or death matter. Stop messing with these fad diets like keto or the alkaline whatever and go on the DASH diet. It's no fad diet. And it most likely won't help you lose weight as fast as you want. But it will help you to halt the progress of the health problems you have that are accelerating fast ... high blood pressure, high cholesterol, and being on the brink of diabetes."

I had watched so many in my family succumb to diabetes. I knew, for them, it was the first of a series of falling dominoes that ended in death.

I decided to become teachable and stop playing Russian roulette with my health.

I took all the meal plans, and allowable and unallowable foods lists home and studied them.

I suddenly realized there would be no need for study or much change really – at all.

In fact, this would be the easiest diet to follow in the world unless I just wanted to be purposefully (and suicidally) rebellious.

Because what was in front of me as unallowable were simply those foods that both me and my subconscious already knew were deadly anyway: doughnuts, snack cakes, prepackaged foods full of salt and sugar, soda pop, candy, cookies - all that stuff we only eat to really punish bodies in the end.

All I had to do was eat what I wanted but stay away from packaged foods full of salt and sugar, watch my oils and opt for heart-healthy options as best I could.

I decided it was time to stop punishing myself, literally. And that has made all the difference in the world.

Enter Forgiveness, Healing, and the Un-Diet DASH Diet!

I decided to forgive myself for years of bad eating and overeating and try it for myself, sticking to the lower recommendations for salt intake and adding in exercise – hand weights and walking 45 minutes 3 days a week.

Soon – well, in 6 months to be exact, I had lost 40 pounds, and my doctor was telling me that my blood markers for both heart disease and diabetes were down. If I continued on my current path, I would avoid a lifelong list of health problems and deadly diagnoses.

So I continued on the DASH diet and upped my days walking to four a week. I got a personal trainer for strength training (and really started to lean down!), and within another six months, I found myself at my current weight of 165 lbs. and still losing.

But It's Really NOT a Diet!

What I love about the DASH diet is it's really not a diet – it's just a healthier way of eating that is still delicious but helps you make all the healthy changes that you want to. And I get to eat my sandwiches. I've just changed out mayonnaise for turkey topped with healthy avocado, tomato, onion, and grainy mustards on 15-grain bread. YUM!

Because you don't feel deprived or have the added stress of deprivation pulling down your energy and mood, you find yourself feeling happier and more alive within days.

Suddenly, you want to do more, be more, eat better, exercise more and be your best self every day! I think this is a combination of avoiding the poison in the SAD (Standard American Diet) and getting all the nutrients you need so that your body, mood, and mind are all in sync - keeping you sane and emotionally healthy enough to stay dedicated to the diet!

I decided to write this book because I want readers to know that you will never feel deprived.

The beauty of the DASH diet is that it's not a restrictive diet at all.

There's nothing you will sacrifice on this diet that you cannot replace with a healthier alternative. You will feel so much better and satisfy your cravings so much more that there's no way you will miss your old diet.

Plus (and this is a big plus), you get to eat sweets.

Yes, the DASH diet never said you could not eat dessert. It says simply to limit your sodium to between 1,500 and 2,300 mg. a day. Vanilla Bean Panna Cotta with Strawberry Sauce. Orange Dream-sickle Cupcakes. Chocolate-Cherry Cookies.

No deprivation!

For example, I had developed this horrible addiction to store-bought cheesecake from the frozen food aisle.

So, I used the DASH diet recipes to create a version with low-fat cream cheese and stevia with real strawberries on top and a dollop of lite whipped cream that is so delicious I never missed the store-bought kind.

That's why the DASH diet works. It doesn't ask you to give up anything – just helps you make healthier – and surprisingly – more delicious choices that your body will thank you for in pounds loss, boundless energy, improved mood, health, and mind for performance!

What Do I Get to Eat - What Do I Give Up?

 With the DASH diet, you still get to eat healthy, whole grain breads freely. In other words, I did not have to give up my beloved sandwiches.

In fact, you do not have to give up healthy bread at all – you simply have to give up the unhealthy kinds and prepackaged foods that are full of dyes, chemicals, bleach, and other life-destroying chemicals.

For every unhealthy thing you have to give up, there is a healthier trade-off that is far more delicious.

For example, instead of conventional, packaged (and therefore loaded with heart-punishing sodium) peaches and cream flavored oatmeal, choose organic, steel-cut oatmeal and add your own organic cream and peaches.

Instead of conventional white bread loaded with chemicals, choose 15-grain whole grain or sprouted bread.

Instead of sweetened vanilla yogurt full of sugar and toxic artificial flavorings, choose unsweetened, organic yogurt flavored with real vanilla beans and topped with berries.

Instead of having a hamburger on a bun with French fries, why not a really tasty steak burger with sweet potato bun and sour cream instead?

Instead of canned vegetable soup - loaded with sodium, BPA, and other hormone-spiking, weight gain causing chemicals - make your own vegetable soup, adding only the least amount of salt that's necessary. Instead, flavor your soup – all your food, in fact -- with adventurous spices that contain no salt but impart a world of flavor.

Some of my favorites are tarragon, garlic, red pepper flakes, peppercorn mixes, and ginger!

In short, there are hardly any unallowable foods on the DASH diet except the nasty guys—trans fats, saturated fats, high sodium, sugar, industrial seed oils, and fast food, which is full of all these things.

With rules like these – which don't seem like rules at all - this is hardly a diet. It's just a way of eating that ensures your health and longevity.

The Importance of Reading Labels

As you can guess by now, you need to look at the labels on your food.

Usually, I'm wasting my time if I'm questioning whether I can eat something and not violate the diet. If it takes that long to scan the label, there are too many fillers and artificial ingredients to call it healthy.

And if your health markers are at an unhealthy point, it's time for healthy, right?

So, that frozen stuffed pastry with chicken and spinach and some kind of tempting white cheese is screaming at you, "I'm loaded with salt, sugar, and a host of unhealthy chemicals and preservatives!"

C'est la vie. If you must have that pastry concoction, we can buy some puff pastry and stuff it with spinach, chopped chicken cooked in white wine, and some Italian white cheese.

It's really best – and time-saving – if you stick to a whole food, clean type of diet that avoids chemicals.

MSG, for example, can spike blood sugar for days, and it's in virtually all fast food. Continuously spiked blood sugar leads to insulin resistance, then obesity and metabolic syndrome, then cardiovascular disease, and the whole deadly cascade of dominoes that follow.

This is why China's diabetes rate is skyrocketing, even though most of the country is thin.

The DASH Diet and The Rainbow

That being said, the DASH diet does encourage you to eat fruits and vegetables often. Think of every week of your journey as one of moving through the colors of the rainbow.

Perhaps one week you can celebrate red fruits and veggies – the following week orange, the next yellow, then green, blue, and purple. Once you get a repertoire of your favorite recipes, you can make eating the rainbow something you do every week, moving through the colors day by day instead of week by week.

Perhaps do green foods twice a week since they're so profoundly healthy for the cardiovascular system.

Plants are loaded with healthy compounds called phytonutrients that scientists know are profoundly healthy but haven't really unlocked the complete science behind them yet. We know it has to do with something called xenohormesis – the plant's defensive compounds to stay alive in drought, decay, or even when prey to munching predators–these are all things we can piggyback on to become more resilient.

In fact, the plant's colors and taste are how they deter predators. They camouflage into the background or manufacture bitter taste. That's why kale tastes so profoundly bitter! But it's also what makes us more resilient in the process.

Allowable and Unallowable Foods

Allowed and Recommended

Whole Grains (6 to 8 servings a day).

Whole grain bread, whole-wheat pasta, whole grain brown or wild rice, popcorn, quinoa, buckwheat, millet, whole steel-cut oats.

Fruits (4 to 5 Servings a Day)

(It is recommended that you, especially by whatever the EWG designates as the Dirty Dozen –organic only. Those chemicals are killers).

Vegetables (5 to 6 servings a day with only 1 starchy vegetable a day, recommended)

(again, consult the Dirty Dozen list and buy these organic).

Lean Proteins

You can eat red meat on the DASH diet, but it is recommended that you eat at most, 2 servings a week. But daily, you can have 6 ounces of lean meat or eggs. A maximum of 6 ounces of lean meat or eggs per day. Vegetarians can opt for tofu and/or tempeh.

- Broiled, roasted, or poached poultry with skin removed
- Eggs
- Fish

Low-fat Dairy

- Fat-free/skim milk
- Low-fat cheese
- Fat-free or low-fat yogurt

Low-Sugar/low fat desserts/sweets

Although the makers of the DASH diet recommend a no-sugar lifestyle, they recognize that everyone needs a treat now and then. Based on your own weight loss goals, you may choose to eat no sweets or limit your intake of low-sugar/low-fat desserts to less than the recommended 5 servings a week.

- Gelatin
- Low-fat ice cream
- Sherbet
- Low-sugar homemade desserts (as always, avoid prepackaged foods full of sodium).

Unallowable foods

- Fast food
- High fat, industrial seed oils
- Lard
- Prepackaged foods high in sugar/sodium/chemicals
- Red meat in excess of 2 six-ounce portions a week
- Table sugar
- Sodium in excess of 2,300 mg. a day.

I've been gathering these recipes over the past 3 years, as I've gotten to know other DASH diet devotees who have shared their favorites with me that were passed down to them by other DASH diet aficionados.

So, if you want the best-tasting food that is super-easy to make and so satisfying, you'll never want to go back to frozen cheesecake and fast food. A whole new world of health awaits you there! Just turn the page.

21 Day Meal Plan

B. Breakfast **L.** Lunch **D.** Dinner

DAY 1	DAY 2	DAY 3	DAY 4	DAY 5	DAY 6	DAY 7
B. Summer Veg Brekkie Cup **L.** Mexican Chicken Salad **D.** Louisiana Turkey Burgers	**B.** Vanilla French Toast with Berry Sauce **L.** Greek Pasta Salad **D.** Haddock Tacos with Mexican Slaw	**B.** Antioxidant Smoothie Bowl **L.** Summer Salmon Parcels **D.** Spicy Enchilada Bake	**B.** Fragrant Shakshuka **L.** Asian Shrimp Salad **D.** Chicken Minestrone	**B.** Avo Trout Toastie **L.** Cheesy Pasta Bake **D.** Pork Poke Bowl	**B.** Veg Breakfast Taco **L.** Tuna and Peach Salad **D.** Spicy Beef Chili	**B.** Colorful Citrus Smoothie **L.** Chili Stuffed Baked Potatoes **D.** Italian Style Rosemary Chicken

DAY 8	DAY 9	DAY 10	DAY 11	DAY 12	DAY 13	DAY 14
B. Raspberry Polenta Waffles **L.** Fancy Pork Fajitas **D.** Lemony Cod with Roast Veg	**B.** Stone Fruit Quinoa **L.** Holiday Waldorf Salad **D.** Peppered Filet with Red wine sauce	**B.** Fruity Breakfast Muffins **L.** Sweet Chili Chicken Wrap **D.** New England Clam Chowder	**B.** Mushroom Frittata **L.** Summer Salmon Parcels **D.** Black Bean Mushroom Burgers	**B.** Sweet Potato and Bean Fry Up **L.** Cheesy Pasta Bake **D.** Mustardy Turkey Meatloaf	**B.** Summer Veg Brekkie Cup **L.** Mexican Chicken Salad **D.** Seafood Paella with Green Veg	**B.** Vanilla French Toast with Berry Sauce **L.** Mexican Chicken Salad **D.** Mustardy Pork Chops

DAY 15	DAY 16	DAY 17	DAY 18	DAY 19	DAY 20	DAY 21
B. Antioxidant Smoothie Bowl **L.** Greek Pasta Salad **D.** Fruity Chicken Curry	**B.** Fragrant Shakshuka **L.** Fancy Pork Fajitas **D.** Cheesy Turkey filled Pasta Shells	**B.** Avo Trout Toastie **L.** Asian Shrimp Salad **D.** Lemony Dorado Tray Bake	**B.** Veg Breakfast Taco **L.** Chili Stuffed Baked Potatoes **D.** Mediterranean Leg of Lamb	**B.** Colorful Citrus Smoothie **L.** Sweet Chili Chicken Wrap **D.** Warming Meaty Soup	**B.** Raspberry Polenta Waffles **L.** Haddock Tacos with Mexican Slaw **D.** Balsamic Roast Chicken	**B.** Stone Fruit Quinoa **L.** Thai Green Soybean Salad **D.** Cajun Crusted Trout

BREAKFAST

SUMMER VEG BREKKIE CUP

PREP TIME: 5 MINS| COOK TIME: 2 MINS | SERVES: 1

INGREDIENTS:

- Unsalted butter or cooking spray, for greasing
- 2 tbsp. fat-free milk
- 2 eggs
- 4 frozen florets broccoli, chopped
- 2 tbsp. sliced button mushrooms
- 2 halved cherry tomatoes
- ¼ cup chard, shredded

- ¼ tsp fresh thyme, chopped
- ½ tsp basil, chopped finely (dried or fresh)
- Black pepper, freshly ground
- 1 tbsp. grated cheese to garnish

DIRECTIONS:

1. Grease a microwave-safe mug with unsalted butter or cooking spray.
2. Making sure not to fill the cup above 2/3 high, add the milk and the eggs, and combine thoroughly using a whisk or a fork.
3. Gently stir in your vegetables, herbs, and pepper to taste.
4. Cook the mug in the microwave on high for 1 minute.
5. Remove mug from the microwave and stir your cup gently, then cook on high for another minute or until the egg is firm and fluffy.
6. Sprinkle with grated cheese to garnish.
7. Serve warm and enjoy!

Quick tips: For a lower-calorie meal, use 1 whole egg, and 2 egg whites. The broccoli can be substituted with cauliflower if you prefer. Other garnishing options are sliced avocado or a spicy tomato salsa.

Per Serving: 177 calories; 6g carbs; 15g protein; 1g fiber; 169mg sodium; 373mg cholesterol; 10g fat

VANILLA FRENCH TOAST WITH BERRY SAUCE

PREP TIME: 10 MINS | COOK TIME: 30 MINS |SERVES: 4

INGREDIENTS:

Berry Sauce:
- 2 and ⅔cups fresh mixed berries
- 1 tbsp. maple syrup
- Fresh lemon juice to taste

French Toast:
- 8 slices of sourdough bread
- ¾ cup 1% milk (low fat)
- 1 large egg and 1 egg white

- ½ teaspoon ground cinnamon
- 1 tbsp. maple syrup
- ½ tsp vanilla extract
- ½ tsp almond essence
- ½ cup toasted almonds, blanched and sliced
- Canola oil for frying
- 1 cup fresh berries to serve

DIRECTIONS:

1. Start by making the sauce. Blend the berries, maple syrup, and lemon juice until smooth. Let sit until needed.

2. Set your oven temperature to 200F.

3. Combine the egg, egg white, and cinnamon in a bowl using a whisk.

4. Then add the milk, maple syrup, vanilla, and almond and whisk until evenly distributed.

5. Oil a non-stick pan using a spray bottle or kitchen brush to thinly coat your pan in Canola oil.

6. Submerge the sliced bread in the egg mixture one at a time. Do not let soak for too long; otherwise, the bread will become soggy and fall apart.

7. Cook each slice on medium-low heat until the sides are evenly browned (about 2 minutes per side).

8. Keep your French toast warm on a tray in the oven until all the slices are done.

9. This dish is best served immediately, with a 3tbsp. of sauce and 2tbsp. toasted almond slices sprinkled over the French toast.

10. Scatter fresh berries over the plate and enjoy!

Quick Tip: Seeded farmhouse bread also works great with this recipe. If you want to keep sugar to a minimum, omit the maple syrup or use a sugar substitute such as erythritol.

Per Serving: 465 Calories; 74g carbs; 16g protein; 16g fiber; 372mg sodium; 49mg cholesterol; 14g fat.

ANTIOXIDANT SMOOTHIE BOWL

PREP TIME: 17 MINS | SERVES: 1

INGREDIENTS:

Smoothie:
- 2 tbsp. chia gel (see step 1)
- ½ medium frozen banana, cut into pieces
- ¾ cup cherries, frozen
- ½ cup coconut yogurt
- 1 tbsp. pure cocoa powder
- 1 tbsp. macadamia nut butter
- 1 cup fresh chard
- 1 teaspoon vanilla extract

- ½ cup unsweetened nut milk.
- 3-4 ice cubes

To serve:
- ½ tbsp. cocoa nibs
- Fresh berries
- Toasted macadamia nuts, roughly chopped
- ½ banana thinly sliced
- Dried goji berries

DIRECTIONS:

1. Make your chia gel first – Mix ⅓cup chia seeds and 2 cups water well. A nice way to do this is to combine the ingredients in a jar and shake it for about 15 seconds. Let the gel rest for 1 minute, then shake/mix again and put it into the fridge for about 10 minutes until it forms a firm gel.

2. Then blend all the smoothie ingredients on high in a blender until you have a beautifully smooth, creamy smoothie. Be sure not to make it too runny by adding the milk little by little

3. Serve topped with the toppings of your choice arranged beautifully, with a sprinkle of cocoa powder to finish.

4. Eat immediately!

Quick tips: You can replace the coconut yogurt with regular low fat plain yogurt. You can also replace the macadamia nut butter and nut milk with any nut butter or alternative milk of your choice; they all taste great. As far as the toppings go, trust your creative instincts, and add any that you think would be delicious.

Per Serving: 412 calories; 61g carbs; 20g protein; 13g fiber; 182mg sodium; 5mg cholesterol; 14g fat

FRAGRANT SHAKSHUKA

PREP TIME: 10 MINS |COOK TIME: 40 MINS | SERVES: 4

INGREDIENTS:

- 1 shallot, diced
- 2 cloves of garlic, finely chopped
- 2 fresh paprika peppers, deseeded and diced
- ½ tsp dried smoked paprika
- ½ tsp dried ground cumin
- 1 tbsp. olive oil
- 28-ounce jar/tin pre-made, low sodium marinara sauce
- 1 cup fresh chard, chopped
- 8 eggs
- ¼ low fat feta cheese
- 1 avocado
- Fresh coriander, finely chopped, to serve
- 2 small focaccia breads, toasted and cut into 8 pieces

DIRECTIONS:

1. Gently fry the shallot, garlic, and fresh paprika in the oil until the shallots are soft.

2. Add the dry spices, and after 1 minute, add your marinara sauce. Gently cook the sauce for approximately 20 min until nicely reduced and flavorful.

3. Add the chard and stir in.

4. Before the chard has time to overcook, make 8 indents in your sauce, using the back of a large spoon. Crack the eggs into each of these indents. Cover the pan with a lid and gently poach the eggs in the sauce for about 6-8 minutes, until the whites are firm and the yolks are done to perfection.

5. Serve with toasted focaccia, crumbled feta, coriander, and sliced avocado. Enjoy hot off the stove!

Quick tips: If you are a spice lover, add 1 tsp of minced red chilies and/or ½ tsp of cayenne pepper when you add your dry spices. You can also swap out the fresh coriander for fresh chopped parsley or even basil.

Per Serving: 454 calories; 45g carbs; 18g protein; 6g fiber; 604mg sodium; 21mg cholesterol; 29g fat.

AVO TROUT TOASTIE

PREP TIME: 5 MINS | COOK TIME: 3 MINS | SERVES: 2

INGREDIENTS:

- 2 Sesame bagels, cut in half
- 1 big avocado,
- 3 ounces cold smoked rainbow trout
- Freshly squeezed lemon juice
- Freshly ground black pepper
- Fresh parsley, shredded
- 2 black cherry tomatoes, cut into slices

DIRECTIONS:

1. Gently toast the bagels under the grill or in a flat pan on a very low heat.

2. While the bagels toast, cut, peel, and pit the avocados, then place in a bowl with a tablespoon of lemon juice, and smash lightly.

3. To serve: smear the avocado evenly over the bagel halves. Lay the tomato slices down, and top with the smoked trout.

4. Finish it off with a generous splash of lemon juice over the fish and some freshly ground black pepper and fresh parsley to taste.

Quick tips: You can substitute the trout for smoked salmon and the black cherry tomatoes for any variety you like. Italian plum tomatoes are also a great option.

Per Serving: 382 calories; 37g carbs; 19g protein; 13g fiber; 490mg sodium; 0mg cholesterol; 20g fat.

VEG BREAKFAST TACO

PREP TIME: 5 MINS | COOK TIME: 7 MINS | SERVES: 2

INGREDIENTS:

- 3 large eggs
- ¼ cup low fat milk
- 1 tbsp. olive oil
- 3 small red, yellow, and green bell peppers, diced
- 1 shallot finely chopped
- 2 cups baby spinach, fresh
- ½ tsp paprika
- Black pepper to taste
- 2 tbsp. crumbled feta cheese
- 2 soft-shell tacos

DIRECTIONS:

1. Whisk together the eggs, milk, paprika, and pepper in a bowl, and set aside.
2. Heat the oil in a pan, then add the shallot and peppers and cook on low heat for about 3 minutes. The onion will go soft and translucent. Then add the baby spinach, turn off the heat, and cover with a lid. Allow spinach to wilt for about 2 minutes.
3. Turn the heat back on and add the egg mixture. Gently stir the eggs until cooked. (About 2 minutes).
4. Serve spooned into the soft-shell tacos and topped with feta cheese.

Quick tips: You can substitute the feta cheese with sliced avocado for a fresher overall meal.

Per Serving: 397 calories; 21g carbs; 16g protein; 11g fiber; 150mg sodium; 0mg cholesterol; 30g fat.

COLORFUL CITRUS SMOOTHIE

PREP TIME: 5 MINS | SERVES: 1

INGREDIENTS:

- ½ cup cooked, sliced beetroot
- ½ cup frozen blueberries
- ½ of 1 Cara Cara orange, peeled and frozen
- ¾ cup unsweetened oat milk
- 1 tbsp. hemp seeds
- 1 tsp honey
- 3 olives

- ½ tsp vanilla essence
- ½ cup low fat Greek yogurt
- 3-4 ice cubes
- ½ tsp guar- and/or xanthan gum

DIRECTIONS:

1. Blend the oat milk and hemp seeds together on low for 20-30 seconds.
2. Then add the remaining ingredients and blend on high until thick, smooth and creamy.

Quick tips: Add ½ tsp of guar gum and/or xanthan gum to your smoothie for an extra-thick finish. You can also substitute the yogurt in this recipe with coconut cream or coconut yogurt for a fully dairy-free smoothie.

Per Serving: 251 calories; 32g carbs; 17g protein; 7g fiber; 239mg sodium; 5mg cholesterol; 6g fat.

RASPBERRY POLENTA WAFFLES

PREP TIME: 15 MINS | COOK TIME: 20 MINS | SERVES: 8

INGREDIENTS:

- 1 tbsp. unsalted butter, melted
- 1 tbsp. sunflower oil
- 1 ¼ cups low fat milk
- 1 cup plain cake flour
- 2 tbsp. caster sugar
- 1 cup finely ground polenta
- 1 ½ tsp baking powder
- 2 large egg whites
- 2 cups low fat, plain yogurt
- 6 ounces raspberries, for serving
- Sunflower oil in a spray bottle for the waffle iron

DIRECTIONS:

1. Mix the milk, oil, and melted butter together in a bowl.
2. Sift the flour, sugar, polenta, and baking powder into a separate bowl, whisk gently, then stir in the milk mixture until just combined. Set aside.
3. Set the oven to 200°F to preheat and turn on your waffle iron to warm up.
4. In an electric mixer, whisk the egg whites until stiff peaks form. Gently fold ⅔ of the egg whites into the flour mixture, add the last ⅓ and fold in.
5. Oil the waffle iron lightly, and then add about 1 cup of the waffle batter into the iron. Close and let cook until they are golden brown and cooked through.
6. To serve, place 2 waffles on a plate stacked on top of each other. Spoon ¼ cup yogurt over them and cascade a handful of raspberries over the top.
7. Enjoy warm!

Quick tips: You can substitute the raspberries for blueberries or strawberries. Polenta is very similar to yellow cornmeal, so you can use that too if you don't have polenta available.

Per Serving: 233 calories; 38g carbs; 9g protein; 2g fiber; 239mg sodium; 10mg cholesterol; 5g fat.

STONE FRUIT QUINOA

PREP TIME: 5 MINS | COOK TIME: 20 MINS | SERVES: 4

INGREDIENTS:

- 1 cup finely chopped fresh apricots
- ½ tsp ground cinnamon
- 2 cups low fat milk
- 1 cup quinoa, rinsed and drained
- 2 tbsp. chopped pecan nuts
- 2 tbsp. honey

DIRECTIONS:

1. Place the apricots, cinnamon, milk, and quinoa in a medium pot, and bring to a boil.
2. Lower the heat slightly and cook for about 20 minutes. The quinoa will absorb most of the liquid by this stage.
3. Turn off the heat and let stand with the lid on for about 5 minutes.
4. Using a fork, incorporate air into the quinoa by whisking gently.
5. Serve hot, with pecans sprinkled over it and a drizzle of honey to sweeten.

Quick tips: Before rinsing your quinoa, check that it hasn't already been pre-rinsed. Some varieties you buy at the shop are.

You can swap out the apricots and nuts for any kind of stone fruit and nut you desire.

Per Serving: 245 calories; 41g carbs; 11g protein; 4g fiber; 81mg sodium; 2mg cholesterol; 5g fat.

FRUITY BREAKFAST MUFFINS

PREP: 15 MINS | COOK TIME: 22 MINS | SERVES: 6

INGREDIENTS:

- 1 cup cake flour
- ½ cup rolled oats
- 1 tsp baking powder
- ½ tsp mixed spice
- 2 ripe bananas
- 1/3 cup castor sugar
- ½ tsp vanilla essence
- ¼ cup sunflower oil
- 1 egg
- Spay and cook
- 1 cup fresh cranberries

DIRECTIONS:

1. Turn the oven on to 350°F to preheat it.

2. Sift together the cake flour, baking powder, and mixed spice in a bowl. Then add the oats.

3. In a separate bowl, mash up the bananas, then add the caster sugar. Mix well, then add the vanilla, oil, and egg and whisk to combine.

4. Mix the dry and wet ingredients in a bowl, then add the cranberries.

5. Spray a 6-cup muffin tray with Spray and Cook, then divide the mixture evenly amongst the muffin cups.

6. Bake for about 20-22 minutes, or until, when a skewer is inserted into the middle, it comes out clean.

7. Yum!

Quick tips: These muffins are great fresh but can last up to 5 days in an airtight container. You can also freeze them for up to 3 months.

You can exchange the cranberries for frozen/fresh blueberries and add half a cup of chopped pecan nuts for that extra nutty goodness.

Per Serving: 305 calories; 47g carbs; 7g protein; 5g fiber; 66mg sodium; 0mg cholesterol; 11g fat.

MUSHROOM FRITTATA

PREP TIME: 10 MINS | COOK TIME: 10 MINS | SERVES: 2

INGREDIENTS:

- 1 tsp unsalted butter, melted
- Spray and Cook
- 1 large brown mushroom, sliced
- ½ cup chopped oyster mushroom
- 2 tbsp. minced onion
- 3 large eggs
- ½ cup sour cream
- Black pepper to taste
- Cherry tomatoes to serve
- 1 sprig basil to serve

DIRECTIONS:

1. Spray a medium non-stick pan with Spray and Cook to prevent any sticking.
2. Add the butter to the pan and fry up the onion and mushrooms gently for 3-4 minutes.
3. Whisk together the eggs and sour cream until well combined. Add black pepper to taste.
4. Turn on the grill function on your oven and allow to heat.
5. Add the egg mixture to the pan and cook gently on low for 2 minutes.
6. Set the pan under the grill for about 1-2 minutes until the top of your frittata is a beautiful golden color.
7. To serve, loosen the edges of the frittata using a spatula. Place a large plate over the top of the pan and then invert it, allowing the frittata to turn over onto the plate.
8. Scatter cherry tomatoes over the top of the frittata and place the basil in the center. Cut and serve warm.

Quick tips: This frittata is great served with a warm slice of buttered toast and grated cheddar cheese.

If you like, you can swap out the mushrooms for 1 small baby marrow, sliced and ½ cup chopped spinach.

Per Serving: 232 calories; 7g carbs; 18g protein; 1g fiber; 329mg sodium; 0mg cholesterol; 15g fat.

SWEET POTATO AND BEAN FRY UP

PREP TIME: 10 MINS | COOK TIME: 10 MINS | SERVES: 3

INGREDIENTS:

- 1 cup sweet potato, washed and diced
- 1 tbsp. olive oil
- 1 tsp ground paprika
- 1 can of red kidney beans- 15 ounces
- 1 cup riced zucchini*
- 2 cups baby spinach finely chopped

- 4 cherry tomatoes halved
- Black pepper to taste
- 1-ounce roasted pumpkin seeds, unsalted
- 1/4 cup fresh coriander, chopped

DIRECTIONS:

1. In a medium-sized pan with high sides, heat the olive oil until a piece of sweet potato placed in the pan sizzles. Add the sweet potato and fry on medium heat for about 5 minutes until browned and cooked through.

2. Then add in the riced zucchini, red kidney beans, paprika, and cherry tomatoes. Cook for about 4 minutes until all the ingredients have heated through. Then add the baby spinach, and wilt for 1 minute. Add black pepper to taste.

3. Serve hot, topped with toasted seeds and chopped herbs.

Quick tips: One can replace the zucchini rice with cauliflower rice, as well as replacing any of the other veg with some of your favorites. *To make the zucchini rice, simply grate one or two zucchinis on the finest side of a grater.

Per Serving: 298 calories; 42g carbs; 14g protein; 12g fiber; 45mg sodium; 0mg cholesterol; 10g fat.

SALADS

MEDLEY OF FRUIT WITH HONEYED RICOTTA

PREP TIME:15 MINS | SERVES: 2

INGREDIENTS:

- ½ a yellow cantaloupe cut into ½ inch pieces
- 1 cup strawberries halved
- 2 crisp Gala apples, peeled, cored, and cut into ½ inch pieces
- 1 large banana, sliced
- 1 lime, quartered
- 1 cup part-skim ricotta cheese
- 2 tsp honey
- 2 sprigs lemon balm mint

DIRECTIONS:

1. Combine all the cut fruit in a bowl, excluding the lime.

2. Squeeze the lime juice over the fruit and then mix to coat the fruit evenly.

3. To serve, spoon the ricotta evenly onto two plates and then pour the honey over the cheese. Cascade the fruit over the ricotta and then garnish with a lime quarter and mint.

Quick tips: Slice the banana last to prevent it from turning brown or replace it with 1 cup blueberries. If desired, you can also replace the ricotta with low-fat cottage cheese and any of the fruit for your favorites.

Per Serving: 500 calories; 89g carbs; 17g protein; 10g fiber; 128mg sodium; omg cholesterol; 11g fat.

MEXICAN CHICKEN SALAD

PREP TIME: 15 MINS | COOK TIME: 45 MINS | SERVES: 6

INGREDIENTS:

Salad:
- 16 ounces skinless chicken breasts, cut into 1-inch cubes
- 1 tbsp. olive oil
- 1 medium white onion, diced
- 1 large fresh paprika pepper, diced
- 1 tbsp. minced garlic
- 1 tsp ground cumin
- 1 tsp dried oregano
- 14.5 ounce can chopped tomatoes (no salt added)
- 1/3 cup water
- 1 large chipotle chili, in adobo sauce, minced

- 15 ounce can black beans, no salt added, drained, and rinsed
- 1 head cos lettuce, shredded
- 6 tbsp. low-fat sour cream
- ½ cup fresh coriander, chopped
- Lime, for serving

Baked Tortilla chips:
- 3 (6-inch) tortilla chips, cut into 24 triangles
- Olive oil, in a pressurized spray bottle

DIRECTIONS:

1. Preheat the oven to 400°F.
2. Heat half the olive oil in a pan and add the chicken cubes. Cook for about 5 minutes until lightly browned. Remove from the pan to drain.
3. Add the remaining oil into the pan, add the onion, garlic, paprika, and fry for about 5 minutes. Add the dried spices and then the canned tomatoes, water, and chipotle. Once this comes up to a simmer, add the chicken, cover, and simmer on low for about 35 minutes, or until the chicken pieces are cooked through.
4. Add the canned beans right at the end of the cooking process, allowing them to heat through for about 5 minutes.
5. Let the chicken chili cool for about 10 minutes.

Tortilla chips

6. Oil a tray using the olive oil spray. Then place the 24 tortilla pieces on the tray and spray the tops of them.
7. Bake in the preheated oven for about 10 minutes, or until crisp and evenly browned. Stir regularly to avoid them burning.

To serve

8. Arrange the lettuce evenly in the center of 6 bowls. Spoon the chili chicken mixture over the lettuce and place 4 tortilla chips per bowl around the edge. Lastly, add 1 tbsp. of sour cream in the center of each bowl, and finish with chopped coriander.
9. Serve warm and enjoy with a dash of lime juice sprinkled over.

Per Serving: 263 calories; 32g carbs; 20g protein; 8g fiber; 484mg sodium; 63mg cholesterol; 10g fat.

SPICY CAULIFLOWER LENTIL SALAD

PREP TIME: 10 MINS| COOK TIME: 25 MINS | SERVES: 4

INGREDIENTS:

- 1 cup lentils
- 1 bay leaf
- 2 tbsp. olive oil
- 1 small red onion, sliced
- 1 large head cauliflower, cut into pieces
- ½ tsp ground ginger
- 1 tsp turmeric powder

- 1 tsp Masala curry powder
- ¼ cup currents
- ¾ cup toasted pecan nuts, chopped roughly
- 8 cups mixed greens (baby lettuce, rocket, baby spinach)
- 1 lime, halved
- ½ cup coriander

DIRECTIONS:

1. Preheat the oven to 400°F.

2. Add the lentils, bay leaf, and enough water (about 2 cups) to cover them in a medium pot and bring to a boil. Let cook until the lentils are al dente (cooked with a slight crunch). Drain the lentils, discard the bay leaf, and leave to cool completely.

3. Combine the cauliflower, olive oil, onion, and spices in a bowl and mix thoroughly to coat the veg. Turn onto a baking tray and bake for about 25 minutes, until golden. Leave to cool.

4. Next, mix together the cooled lentils, cauliflower, currents, and nuts in a bowl.

5. To serve, place a handful of greens in the center of your serving plate and spoon the cauliflower mixture onto the middle. Garnish with coriander and a generous squeeze of lime juice.

6. Enjoy!

Quick tips: Be sure not to crowd the cauliflower when roasting it; otherwise, it won't brown well. You could swap out the brown lentils for black lentils or even mung beans and replace the pecan nuts with any nut of your choice.

Per Serving: 437 calories; 53g carbs; 22g protein; 23g fiber; 141mg sodium; 0mg cholesterol; 22g fat.

NUTTY ARTICHOKE SALAD

PREP TIME: 15 MINS | COOK TIME: 20 MINS | SERVES: 2 to 3

INGREDIENTS:

For the dressing
- 5 tsp grape seed oil
- 2 tsp white wine vinegar
- ¼ tsp sugar
- 1tsp finely chopped parsley

For the salad
- 6 cleaned and cooked artichoke hearts (8-ounce jar)
- ½ cup chopped, toasted almonds
- 3 cups mixed green leaves
- ¼ cup olive oil
- 5 small, sweet peppers, sliced

DIRECTIONS:

1. Preheat the oven to 450°F.

2. First, make the dressing. Whizz the dressing ingredients together in a blender until well blended. Set aside until serving.

3. Place the peppers on a baking tray and drizzle the olive oil over them. Toss to coat them evenly and then roast them for 20 minutes until they have a good amount of color. Leave to cool completely.

4. To assemble the salad, divide the greens between either two or three bowls, arrange the artichokes and peppers on top of the greens. Sprinkle the toasted nuts over the salad and then drizzle the dressing over generously.

5. Serve immediately and enjoy!

Quick tips: For extra protein in the salad, add ½ cup cooked chicken or chickpeas to the salad.

Per Serving: 645 calories; 29g carbs; 11g protein; 10g fiber; 89mg sodium; 0mg cholesterol; 58g fat.

HOLIDAY WALDORF SALAD

PREP TIME: 15 MINS | SERVES: 4

INGREDIENTS:

- 10 ounces cooked turkey breast, cut into cubes
- 2 sweet red apples diced into ½ inch squares
- ¼ cup dried sultanas
- ¼ cup unsalted raw pumpkin seeds
- 2 tbsp. diced celery
- ¼ cup sour cream
- 2 tbsp. mayonnaise
- ¼ tsp ground black pepper
- 5 ounces mixed greens
- 1 sprig parsley to garnish

DIRECTIONS:

1. Mix the turkey, apples, sultanas, seeds, and celery in a bowl.

2. In another small bowl, whisk together the sour cream, mayonnaise, and black pepper. Then add this mixture to the turkey bowl and stir in evenly.

3. Serve on a bed of mixed greens and garnish with a sprig of parsley and enjoy immediately.

Quick tips: Before adding the mixed greens, the turkey mayonnaise mixture can be stored in the fridge for up to 1 day.

Per Serving: 233 calories; 22 carbs; 20g protein; 4g fiber; 215mg sodium; 47mg cholesterol; 8g fat.

THAI GREEN SOYBEAN SALAD

PREP TIME: 10 MINS |COOK TIME: 2 MINS | SERVES: 4

INGREDIENTS:

- ¼ cup smooth peanut butter
- 1 ½ tsp minced ginger
- ½ tsp minced garlic
- ½ tsp minced fresh chili
- 2 tbsp. apple cider vinegar
- 2 tbsp. fresh lemon juice
- 1 tsp low sodium soya sauce
- 1 tbsp. honey
- Boiling water

- 1 16-ounce packet of frozen green soybeans
- 2 cup red cabbage, cut chiffonade style
- 2 cups Chinese cabbage, cut chiffonade style
- 4 medium radishes, sliced in thin discs
- 1 cup carrot, cut julienne style
- 1 sweet red pepper, sliced thinly
- ¼ small red onion, finely sliced
- ½ cup fresh coriander

DIRECTIONS:

1. Make the dressing first by placing the peanut butter, vinegar, lemon juice, soya sauce, honey, minced ginger, garlic, and chili in a small bowl. Add one tbsp. of boiling water at a time until the dressing is a good pouring consistency.

2. Cook the soybeans per the directions on the packet. Usually, one submerges the beans in boiling water for 1-2 minutes. Be sure not to add any salt to your cooking water. Allow to cool.

3. Mix all the chopped vegetables and the cooled soybeans in a bowl. Then add the dressing and toss well to coat the salad evenly.

4. Stir in the coriander just before serving.

Quick tips: Green soybeans are also known as Edamame beans, so be on the lookout for those when doing your shopping. To lower the sodium levels in this salad even further, one can replace the soy sauce with balsamic vinegar.

Per Serving: 223 calories; 22g carbs; 12g protein; 7g fiber; 101mg sodium; 0mg cholesterol; 10g fat.

TUNA AND PEACH SALAD

PREP TIME: 15 MINS | COOK TIME: 21 MINS | SERVES: 2

INGREDIENTS:

- 6 small sweet red/yellow peppers whole
- 2 6-ounce tuna steaks
- 3 tbsp. olive oil
- 2 tbsp. balsamic vinegar
- 1 ½ lemons, juiced
- 4 cups fresh rocket

- ¼ cup fresh basil
- Black pepper to taste
- 2 large white flesh dessert peaches, cut into cubes
- 1 lemon, quartered, to serve

DIRECTIONS:

1. Marinate the tuna steaks first. Mix 1 tbsp. olive oil, balsamic vinegar, and the juice of half a lemon together in a bowl. Add the steaks and turn them over to coat on all sides. Set aside.

2. Preheat the oven to 450°F. Set it onto the grill function.

3. Place the peppers under the grill whole and grill for about 10-15 minutes. Turn the peppers over at least twice during this time. The skin should start to blister and char slightly. Cut them in half, remove the seeds and stalks, cut into chunks, drizzle with 1 tsp of olive oil, and put aside to cool.

4. Heat a grill pan or non-stick pan and cook the tuna on high heat for 3 minutes on each side. Remove from the heat and then slice. Keep warm until serving, either in tin foil or a casserole dish in the oven at the lowest temperature.

5. Whisk together the remaining lemon juice and olive oil. Add the rocket and basil to a bowl and dress lightly with this lemon juice mixture.

6. To serve, divide the greens between two plates and top with the peppers, peaches, and warm tuna, in that order. Season with black pepper, and place 1-2 lemon quarters on the plate.

7. Squeeze over a little lemon juice and enjoy!

Quick tips: You can replace the peaches with 1 large mango for a more tropical feel. Alternatively, if you prefer a more savory taste, replace the peaches with 1 ounce of crumbled feta and 2 tbsp. sliced calamata olives.

Per Serving: 511 calories; 50g carbs; 32g protein; 6g fiber; 67mg sodium; 0mg cholesterol; 23g fat.

ASIAN SHRIMP SALAD

PREP TIME: 10 MINS | COOK TIME: 3 MINS | SERVES: 2

INGREDIENTS:

- 2 tbsp. minced fresh ginger
- 1tsp low sodium soy sauce
- ¼ tsp ground dried chili
- 1 tbsp. grapeseed oil
- ½ tsp sesame seed oil
- 2 tbsp. apple cider vinegar
- 8-ounces shrimp, cooked, deveined, peeled, and cubed
- 1 cup coarsely grated carrots
- ¼ roasted, chopped cashew nuts - unsalted

- 1 medium sweet red pepper, sliced
- 2 tbsp. diced spring onions
- 1 cup fresh snow peas, topped and tailed and halved
- 6 cups mixed baby Asian greens

DIRECTIONS:

1. In a glass measuring jug, mix the salad dressing ingredients: ginger, soy sauce, chili, grapeseed oil, sesame oil, and apple cider vinegar. Whisk lightly to combine. Set aside.

2. Place the shrimp, carrots, nuts, peppers, and spring onion in a bowl.

3. Bring a small pot of water to a boil and lightly blanch the snow peas for 1-2 minutes. They should remain a vibrant green color and retain some of their crunch. Run under cold water to cool them and prevent them from cooking any further.

4. Once cooled, add the peas to the bowl with the shrimps and vegetables in, and pour over the dressing. Stir gently with a spoon.

5. Place half the Asian greens onto each plate and divide the shrimp mixture between the two. Place the shrimp in the center of your greens and serve immediately.

6. Enjoy!

Per Serving: 403 calories; 23g carbs; 32g protein; 9g fiber; 568mg sodium; 221mg cholesterol; 18g fat.

NAVAL TUNA SALAD

PREP TIME: 10 MINS | SERVES: 2

INGREDIENTS:

- 1 cup cooked Navy beans, rinsed
- 2.6-ounce can of tuna, low sodium
- 2 tbsp. finely chopped onion
- ¼ cup diced red sweet pepper
- 1tsp minced fresh garlic
- 1 ½ tsp fresh lemon juice
- 3 tbsp. low fat Greek yogurt

- 1tbsp. olive oil
- 2 tsp fresh dill, finely chopped, plus extra for serving
- Fresh black pepper to taste
- 2 cups fresh rocket

DIRECTIONS:

1. Mix the beans, tuna, onion, and red pepper in a bowl.

2. Then make the dressing - whisk together the garlic, lemon juice, olive oil, dill, and Greek yogurt.

3. Combine the tuna mixture with the dressing and mix well.

4. Place 1 cup of rocket on each plate and spoon the tuna mixture into the center.

5. Garnish with a sprig or two of dill and enjoy.

Quick tips: You can replace the Navy beans with cooked cannellini beans if you like. Just make sure whatever beans you use, you cook without salt, or buy the low sodium cans. Rinsing the canned beans can drastically reduce the sodium content even further.

Per Serving: 229 calories; 25g carbs; 17g protein; 9g fiber; 267mg sodium; 17mg cholesterol; 7g fat.

GREEK PASTA SALAD

PREP TIME: 35 MINS | COOK TIME: 9 MINS | SERVES: 3

INGREDIENTS:

- ⅓ cup pasta rice, uncooked
- 1 medium Ashley cucumber, peeled, deseeded, and diced
- 1 cup yellow plum tomatoes, halved
- ¼ cup pitted black olives
- 2 tbsp. grapeseed oil
- 1 tbsp. fresh lime juice
- 1 tsp finely chopped fresh garlic

- Freshly ground black pepper to taste
- 2 tbsp. fresh basil, lightly chopped
- 3 tbsp. fresh flat-leaf parsley, plus 3 extra sprigs to garnish
- 2 ounces reduced-fat crumbled ricotta cheese

DIRECTIONS:

1. Fill a small pot ¾ of the way with water and bring it to a boil. Add the pasta rice and cook until al dente, about 9 minutes.

2. Once cooked, rinse the pasta rice with cold water, and then allow it to cool completely for about 20 minutes.

3. While it cools, whisk together the grapeseed oil, lemon juice, garlic, basil, and black pepper to make the dressing.

4. Mix the cucumber, tomatoes, olives, and parsley with the cooled pasta rice and then pour ¾ of the dressing over and mix well.

5. To serve, divide the pasta rice mixture evenly among the plates, sprinkle over the crumbled ricotta and then drizzle the remaining ¼ of the dressing over the ricotta.

6. Garnish with parsley sprig and enjoy.

Quick tips: Pasta Rice is also known as Orzo. Keep that in mind when looking for it in the shops. For a more authentic Greek dish, use crumbled low-fat feta instead of the ricotta.

Per Serving: 232 calories; 21g carbs; 5g protein; 2g fiber; 262 sodium; 0mg cholesterol; 14g fat.

HERBED MUNG BEAN SALAD

PREP TIME: 15 MINS | COOK TIME: 35 MINS | SERVES: 6

INGREDIENTS:

- 2 tbsp. red wine vinegar
- Zest of 2 medium limes
- 2 tbsp. extra virgin olive oil
- 2 tbsp. water
- Freshly ground black pepper to taste
- ¼ tsp celery salt - no sodium
- 1 cup mung beans, rinsed

- 2 pieces celery, diced
- 2 medium fresh paprika peppers, chopped into cubes
- 1 medium carrot, peeled and diced
- 1 cup crumbled goats chevre
- 1 tsp finely chopped parsley
- 1 tsp finely chopped basil, plus extra sprigs to garnish
- ½ tsp finely chopped oregano
- ½ tsp finely chopped lemon thyme

DIRECTIONS:

1. Bring a medium pot of water to a boil.

2. While waiting for it to boil, make the dressing by combining the red wine vinegar, lime zest, water, celery salt, and black pepper in a bowl, then slowly whisking in the olive oil. Set aside.

3. Add the mung beans to boiling water and cook for 30-40 minutes until soft but not mushy. Run under cold water and set aside to cool.

4. Once cooled, add the chopped vegetables and herbs, and pour the dressing over. Mix well.

5. To serve, spoon salad into a bowl, and cascade the crumbled chevre over it. Garnish with a sprig of basil.

6. Serve chilled.

Quick tips: You can swap out the mung beans for green lentils. This salad can be stored in the fridge for a maximum of one day. If you want to store and serve it later, keep ¼ of the dressing aside to refresh the salad just before serving.

Per Serving: 170 calories; 22g carbs; 9g protein; 11g fiber; 21mg sodium; 0mg cholesterol; 5g fat.

POULTRY

ITALIAN STYLE ROSEMARY CHICKEN

PREP TIME: 10 MINS | COOK TIME: 25 MINS | SERVES: 4

INGREDIENTS:

- 2 tsp corn flour
- 1 cup low sodium chicken stock
- 2 12-ounce chicken breasts, cut in half and lightly tenderized to an even thickness
- 1 tbsp. olive oil, plus extra in a spray bottle
- ½ white onion, diced
- ¼ tsp fresh black pepper

- 2 small fresh paprika peppers, finely chopped
- 1 14.5-ounce can chopped tomatoes, low sodium
- 1 tsp minced fresh garlic
- 9-ounces fresh asparagus, blanched and drained
- 2 tsp fresh rosemary finely chopped
- ¼ tsp minced fresh chili

DIRECTIONS:

1. Using the spray bottle, oil a non-stick pan and heat. Brown the 4 chicken pieces in the oil for about 6 minutes per side.

2. Remove the chicken from the pan and heat 1 tbsp. of olive oil in it. Fry off the onion, paprika and garlic for about 5 minutes. Pour in the tomatoes and then add the stock mixture, making sure to give a stir first to loosen any flour particles.

3. Add the rosemary, chili and chicken and bring to a slow boil. Cover, and cook on a gentle heat for about 6 minutes until the chicken is cooked through and the sauce thick.

4. Add the asparagus in the last 2 minutes of cooking to heat through.

5. Serve hot and enjoy!

Quick tips: You can replace the asparagus with a 9-ounce can of artichoke hearts.

Per Serving: 300 calories; 15g carbs; 40g protein; 5g fiber; 534mg sodium; 109mg cholesterol; 9g fat.

NUT-CRUSTED CHICKEN

PREP TIME: 10 MINS | COOK TIME: 25 MINS | SERVES: 4

INGREDIENTS:

- 4 4-ounce chicken breasts, deboned and skin removed
- 1 tbsp. olive oil
- 1 tsp ground cayenne pepper
- ½ tsp ground black pepper
- ½ cup pecan nuts
- ½ cup flax seeds, ground into meal
- 4 cups green beans, topped and tailed and cut in half
- 1 lemon, cut into quarters

DIRECTIONS:

1. Lightly oil a baking tray using an oil brush.
2. Preheat the oven to 350°F and then blitz the nuts in a blender to form a meal.
3. Mix the ground nuts, flax meal, cayenne pepper, and black pepper. Then put this mixture into a bag. It can be a resealable plastic one or a brown paper bag.
4. Add the chicken breasts to the bag, make sure it is well sealed at the top and give it a good shake. Make sure to coat all the sides of the chicken with the crust mixture.
5. Place the crusted chicken pieces on the baking tray and bake for about 25-30 minutes or until a food thermometer reads 165 °F at the center of the chicken. Discard the remaining crust mixture.
6. Bring a small pot of water to a boil.
7. 5 minutes before the chicken is cooked, blanch the green beans in boiling water, cooking them until still crunchy and bright green. Drain off the water.
8. Serve the chicken hot alongside the beans and finish it off with a lemon quarter.

Quick tips: You can substitute the green beans for any vegetable of your choosing. Broccoli is also an excellent option. Another substitution could be the pecan nuts, which you could swap out for any nut of your choosing.

Per Serving: 310 calories; 14g carbs; 31g protein; 8g fiber; 308mg sodium; 55mg cholesterol; 18g fat.

SWEET CHILI CHICKEN WRAP

PREP TIME: 15 MINS | SERVES: 4

INGREDIENTS:

- 4 large wholegrain wraps
- 2/3 cup sweet chili mayonnaise mixture, store-bought
- 2 cups cooked pulled chicken breast
- ¼ cup white cabbage, cut chiffonade style
- 2 spring onions, sliced
- ¼ cup grated carrot
- ¼ cucumber, peeled, deseeded, and thinly shaved with a peeler
- 2 tbsp. fresh coriander, chopped
- 2 small avocados, cut into cubes
- Spray bottle of olive oil

DIRECTIONS:

1. Lightly coat the cooked chicken in ⅓ cup of sweet chili mayonnaise. Then, in a bowl, mix the chicken, cabbage, onion, carrot, cucumber, coriander, and avocado together.

2. Divide the mixture into 4 and roll the wraps, making sure to fold over the ends to prevent the mixture from falling out.

3. Heat a non-stick pan, lightly spray with oil, and then toast the wraps lightly on all sides until golden brown.

4. Cut in half and serve warm with the remaining ⅓cup sweet chili mayonnaise.

Quick tips: If you'd like to make your own sauce for this recipe, mix ½ cup yogurt, 2 tbsp. mayonnaise, lemon juice and pepper to taste and 1 tsp Dijon mustard together.

Another great sauce option is a spicy Asian style peanut sauce. Other things you could add to the wrap are chopped celery, nuts, cranberries, and cherry tomato halves.

Per Serving: 228 calories; 19g carbs; 31g protein; 9g fiber; 368mg sodium; 60mg cholesterol; 5g fat.

AVO CHICKEN TACOS

PREP TIME: 15 MINS | COOK TIME: 15 MINS | SERVES: 2

INGREDIENTS:

- 2 Roma tomatoes, cut into cubes
- 1 tbsp. chopped fresh coriander, plus extra for garnishing
- 1 tsp garlic, minced
- 1 sweet pepper, cut into cubes
- ½ cup white onion, diced
- 1 tsp virgin olive oil
- 9-ounces skinless chicken breast cut into cubes
- ½ tsp ground cumin
- ½ tsp ground paprika
- ½ tsp dried oregano
- ½ tsp ground dried chili
- ½ tsp ground dried coriander
- ¼ cup water
- 1 lime, cut into 4
- 4 hard shell tacos
- 1 avocado, diced
- ½ cup low fat sour cream

DIRECTIONS:

1. Mix the tomatoes and coriander in a bowl and set aside.

2. Next, fry the onion, peppers, and garlic in the olive oil until cooked. Then remove from the pan, retaining as much of the oil as possible in the pan.

3. Add the chicken pieces to the pan and fry for 2 minutes. Then add all the spices and stir well. Add the water and squeeze one of the lime quarter's juices into the pan.

4. Cook the chicken for about 5 minutes, or until cooked through. Turn off the heat and add the pepper mixture into the pan.

5. While the chicken cooks, heat the taco shells in the oven for about 5 minutes.

6. To assemble, spoon the chicken mixture and tomato mixture out evenly between the tacos. Divide the diced avocado between the tacos, then drop a spoon of sour cream on top and garnish with a sprig of coriander and lime quarters.

Per Serving: 346 calories; 30g carbs; 32g protein; 4g fiber; 150mg sodium; 0mg cholesterol; 11g fat

GARLICKY ASIAN CHICKEN

PREP TIME: 5 MINS | COOK TIME: 15 MINS | SERVES: 4

INGREDIENTS:

- 17 ounces chicken breast, without skins, and cut into cubes
- 4 tsp sunflower oil
- 1 tbsp. low sodium soy sauce
- 1 tsp brown sugar
- 2 tbsp. apple cider vinegar
- ¾ cup low sodium chicken stock
- ½ tsp chili powder
- 2 tsp corn flour

- 3 tbsp. finely chopped garlic
- 2 tbsp. finely chopped fresh ginger
- 3 spring onion, sliced
- 2 heads of tatsoi, roughly chopped

DIRECTIONS:

1. First, heat 2 tsp oil in a pan, and fry off the chicken pieces to brown for about 2 minutes. Remove chicken from the pan and place in a bowl to retain juices.

2. Make up the sauce by whisking together the soy sauce, sugar, vinegar, stock chili powder and lastly, the corn flour. Mix well to combine and then set aside.

3. Next, start frying the ginger and garlic in the last 2 tsp oil. Add the onion for about 2 minutes, then add the tatsoi and cook for another minute. Add the chicken and juices and cook for a further minute.

4. Lastly, add the sauce and bring to a boil, cooking until the chicken is cooked through and the sauce thick and sticky.

5. Serve immediately and enjoy.

Quick tips: Sliced shitake mushrooms are a delicious additive to this recipe. Add them in at the same time as the spring onions.

Per Serving: 225 calories; 10g carbs; 28g protein; 2g fiber; 409mg sodium; 72mg cholesterol; 8g fat.

BALSAMIC ROAST CHICKEN

PREP TIME: 40 MINS | COOK TIME: 35 MINS | SERVES: 2

INGREDIENTS:

- 2 4-ounce skinless chicken breasts
- Fresh black pepper to taste
- 1 tsp finely chopped fresh garlic
- 1 tbsp. fresh thyme chopped
- 1 tsp grapeseed oil
- ½ cup balsamic vinegar, plus 2 tbsp. extra

- 8-ounces broccoli florets
- 2 tsp balsamic vinegar
- 2 tsp grapeseed oil
- Freshly ground black pepper to taste
- 2 tbsp. toasted cashew nuts
- Sprigs fresh parsley to garnish

DIRECTIONS:

1. Place the ½ cup balsamic vinegar, garlic, pepper, thyme, and oil in a small pot and bring to a boil. Simmer for about 3 minutes or until the liquid has reduced by about half.

2. Cool this mixture in the freezer for 5 minutes.

3. Oil a baking tray and place the chicken on it. Cover the chicken in the cooled marinade and leave to chill for 30 minutes.

4. Meanwhile, preheat the oven to 375 °F.

5. Mix the broccoli florets with 2 tsp balsamic vinegar, 2 tsp grapeseed oil, and pepper. Oil a second baking tray and lay the veg out on it.

6. After 30 minutes, cover the marinated chicken with foil and place in the oven to roast for 30-35 minutes.

7. For the last 15-20 minutes, place the broccoli in the oven to roast too. Give them a good stir at least once while cooking.

8. Once the chicken is cooked, serve it hot with the broccoli on the side, topped with toasted cashews and garnished with a sprig of parsley.

Quick tips: You can swap out the broccoli for Brussel sprouts and use rosemary in the recipe instead of fresh thyme.

Per Serving: 304 calories; 23g carbs; 28g protein; 5g fiber; 556mg sodium; 55mg cholesterol; 12g fat.

SPICY CHICKEN MAC N CHEESE

PREP TIME: 10 MINS | COOK TIME: 26 MINS | SERVES: 4

INGREDIENTS:

- 8 ounces macaroni pasta
- 1 tbsp. flour
- 1 tbsp. unsalted butter
- 2 cups low fat milk
- Olive oil in a spray bottle
- ½ cup finely chopped white onion
- ¼ low fat mascarpone cheese
- ¼ tsp garlic powder
- Black pepper to taste

- 2 tbsp. Buffalo hot sauce, plus extra to serve
- 12 ounces cooked pulled chicken breast
- 2 tbsp. feta crumbled feta cheese
- ½ cup grated mature cheddar cheese

DIRECTIONS:

1. Bring a medium pot of water to a boil. Add the pasta and cook for about 9 minutes, or until al dente. Drain and cover to keep warm.

2. Next, make your white sauce. Melt the butter in a small pot, then add the four and whisk vigorously to prevent lumps from forming. Gradually add the milk, whisking all the time. After 2 minutes, add the mascarpone, garlic powder and pepper and stir for another 3 minutes.

3. Meanwhile, fry off the onion until soft using a little olive oil.

4. Then add the Buffalo sauce, grated cheese, and feta to the sauce. Stir for 1 minute, and lastly, add in the onions.

5. Bring the dish together by adding the pulled chicken and pasta into the sauce and stirring well.

6. Spoon into serving bowls hot and serve with additional buffalo sauce

Quick tips: If your sauce is too runny, add 2 tbsp. more mascarpone to thicken it.

Per Serving: 541 calories; 52g carbs; 44g protein; 2g fiber; 537mg sodium; 0mg cholesterol; 16g fat.

MUSTARDY TURKEY MEATLOAF

PREP TIME: 15 MINS | COOK TIME: 50 MINS | SERVES: 4

INGREDIENTS:

- 1 shallot diced
- 1 medium carrot finely chopped
- 3 tbsp. diced celery
- 2 tsp olive oil, plus extra in a spray bottle
- 1 tsp finely chopped thyme
- 18-ounces minced turkey meat
- ¾ cup rice bran

- 1 egg, beaten
- 1 tsp finely chopped parsley
- Black pepper to taste
- 1 tsp yellow mustard
- 1 tbsp. honey

DIRECTIONS:

1. Heat 2 tsp olive oil in a pan and fry off the shallot, carrot, celery, and thyme until soft and cooked.

2. Preheat the oven to 350°F.

3. Mix the mustard and honey and set aside.

4. In a bowl, mix the turkey mince, rice bran, egg, and parsley. Then add the shallot mixture and mix well—season with black pepper to taste.

5. Shape the mixture into 4 small meatloaves of about 5x3 inches in size. Place them on an oiled baking tray and bake for about 35 minutes. Remove from the oven and baste with the mustard mixture. Return them to the oven for a further 5 minutes for glazing.

6. Before serving and slicing, allow the loaves to rest for 5 minutes.

7. Serve hot with any remaining honey mustard sauce.

Per Serving: 335 calories; 21g carbs; 32g protein; 3g fiber; 484mg sodium; 147mg cholesterol; 15g fat.

CRISPY TURKEY IN TOMATO SAUCE

PREP TIME: 5 MINS: | COOK TIME: 20 MINS | SERVES: 4

INGREDIENTS:

- 2 tbsp. olive oil
- ½ small onion, minced
- 2 tsp garlic, finely chopped
- 1 medium carrot, grated
- 1 large sweet red pepper, sliced
- 1 cup pink oyster mushrooms, sliced

- 1 tsp dried thyme
- 1 14.5-ounce low sodium can chopped tomatoes
- 17-ounces turkey breast - 4 breasts
- Sprig parsley to garnish

DIRECTIONS:

1. First, make your tomato sauce by heating 1 tbsp. oil in a pan. Add in the onion, garlic, carrot, and pepper. Fry for about 1 minute. Then add in the dried thyme and oyster mushrooms. Lastly, add in the canned tomatoes, and simmer on low heat for about 7 minutes.

2. In a separate pan, fry off the turkey breasts in the remaining oil. Cook for about 3 minutes on each side until cooked through and a crisp brown outer layer is formed.

3. Add the turkey breasts and juices to the sauce and simmer for about 2 minutes to amalgamate the flavors.

4. Serve hot, garnished with a sprig of parsley.

Quick tips: Replacing the thyme in the recipe with tarragon makes for an equally delicious meal.

Per Serving: 225 calories; 10g carbs; 30g protein; 2g fiber; 67mg sodium; 70mg cholesterol; 8g fat.

CHEESY TURKEY FILLED PASTA SHELLS

PREP TIME: 20 MINS | COOK TIME: 50 MINS | SERVES: 2-3

INGREDIENTS:

- 8 large individual pasta shells
- ½ tsp olive oil, plus extra in a spray bottle
- ¼ cup finely chopped red onion
- 1 tsp fresh garlic, minced
- 8-ounces turkey mince, lean
- 1 cup grated gouda cheese
- 1 ½ cups low fat cream cheese
- Black pepper to taste
- 2 tbsp. finely chopped parsley
- 8-ounces Swiss chard, de-stemmed and roughly chopped
- 1 ½ cups readymade Marinara sauce

DIRECTIONS:

1. Bring a medium pot of water to a boil.

2. Preheat the oven to 375^{0}F and spray a semi-deep casserole dish with olive oil.

3. Place the pasta shells in boiling water and cook for about 8 minutes. Drain and place on the greased casserole dish.

4. Heat the oil in a pan, and fry off the onion, with the garlic and black pepper to taste. Once the onions are soft, add in the turkey mince, and cook until it changes color completely, about 6 minutes. Add the Swiss chard in the last minutes and turn off the heat.

5. In a bowl, mix the cream cheese with all but 3 tbsp. Gouda. Add in the parsley and then the turkey mixture and mix well. Season with pepper to taste.

6. Place ½ cup of marinara sauce underneath the pasta shells in the casserole dish. Then fill them equally with the turkey mixture. Pour the rest of the marinara sauce over them and cover with grated cheese.

7. Bake covered for 25 minutes, uncover, and bake for another 5 minutes until the cheese browns nicely.

8. Serve hot and enjoy.

Quick tips: This dish freezes well for up to 3 months.

Per Serving: 907 calories; 73g carbs; 70g protein; 8g fiber; 714mg sodium; 0mg cholesterol; 39g fat.

LOUISIANA TURKEY BURGERS

PREP TIME: 45 MINS | COOK TIME: 17 MINS | SERVES: 4

INGREDIENTS:

- ½ cup apple cider vinegar
- 1 small red onion, thinly sliced
- 2 tsp olive oil, plus extra in a spray bottle
- 20-ounces turkey mince
- 2 small shallots, diced
- 1 small sweet paprika pepper, cut into cubes
- 2 tsp minced fresh garlic
- 4 tbsp. finely chopped fresh parsley

- 1 stalk celery, diced
- 1 tsp readymade Cajun spice mix
- 4 whole Ciabatta burger buns
- ¼ cup low fat mayonnaise
- 1 tsp Dijon mustard
- 1 cup rocket leaves
- 4 slices Roma tomato

DIRECTIONS:

1. Cover the sliced red onion in vinegar and set aside to pickle for between 30 minutes to 6 hours.

2. Heat 2 tsp oil, add the shallots, garlic, Cajun spice, paprika, and celery and fry for 2 minutes until vegetables are soft.

3. Mix the mince, parsley, and cooled onion mixture. Shape 4 burgers out of the mixture, put in the fridge for 15 minutes to rest.

4. Spray a non-stick pan with olive oil, then fry the burgers for 5 minutes a side, until golden brown and cooked through.

5. Stir together the mayonnaise and mustard.

6. Assemble the burgers by cutting the buns in half, spreading evenly with mustard mayo, place rocket and tomatoes on the bottom half. Place the burgers on top of the tomatoes and finish off with a small spoon of pickled onion and bun top. Serve hot.

7. Get the serviettes ready and enjoy.

Per Serving: 420 calories; 36g carbs; 33g protein; 6g fiber; 698mg sodium; 105mg cholesterol; 17g fat.

SEAFOOD

ITALIAN STYLE PARMESAN SCALLOPS

PREP TIME: 45 MINS | COOK TIME: 30 MINS | SERVES: 4

INGREDIENTS:

- 35-ounces sea scallops
- 2 spring onions, finely chopped
- 1 bay leaf
- ¼ cup dry white wine
- ½ cup olive oil
- 2 tbsp. unsalted butter
- 1 ½ tbsp. corn flour
- ¾ cup low fat milk

- ¼ grated Gruyere cheese
- Black pepper to taste
- ¼ cup grated parmesan
- 1 tbsp. breadcrumbs

DIRECTIONS:

1. Heat the olive oil in a pan and fry the scallops for 5-7 minutes. Drain off any liquid and set aside until needed.

2. Next, make a wine stock by bringing the wine, spring onions, and bay leaf to a boil. Boil until the liquid is reduced by half. Strain the mixture and discard the onion and bay leaf, keeping only the wine stock.

3. Preheat the oven to 400°F.

4. Melt the butter in a small pot, then whisk in the corn flour to prevent lumps forming. Gradually add in the milk and wine stock, whisking all along. Once this mixture thickens, add black pepper to taste. Add the Gruyere cheese and stir until thick.

5. Remove sauce from the heat. Place the scallops in a greased baking dish, then pour the sauce over them. Top with the breadcrumbs and parmesan to form a crust.

6. Bake for about 15 minutes until well browned and serve hot.

Quick tips: Leftovers can be stored for up to 3 days in a fridge. Scallops can be replaced with chicken pieces.

Per Serving: 342 calories; 16g carbs; 33g protein; 1g fiber; 423mg sodium; 0mg cholesterol; 12g fat.

HADDOCK TACOS WITH MEXICAN SLAW

PREP TIME: 10 MINS | COOK TIME: 8 MINS | SERVES: 6

INGREDIENTS:

- Olive oil in a spray bottle
- 12-ounces cabbage cut chiffonade style
- 2 tbsp. low fat sour cream
- 2 tbsp. fresh lime juice
- Zest of 1 lime
- 1 small red pepper, sliced
- 2 spring onions finely sliced

- 2 tbsp. chopped fresh coriander, plus extra to garnish
- 2 tbsp. minced fresh mint
- 24-ounces haddock fillets
- 2 tsp cayenne pepper
- 2 tbsp. fresh lime juice
- 12 6-inch hard shell corn tacos
- 2 limes cut into quarters to serve

DIRECTIONS:

1. Mix the sour cream, lime juice and zest in a large bowl. Add the cabbage, red pepper, onions, mint, and coriander and combine.

2. In a separate bowl, combine the other 2 tbsp. lime juice and cayenne pepper. Pour this mixture over the fish fillets and let stand in the fridge for 2 minutes.

3. Oil a non-stick pan and fry the haddock until flaky and cooked through. About 9 minutes a side.

4. Place in a bowl and pull apart into pieces. Mix in the cabbage mixture.

5. Warm the tacos in oven for about 2 minutes, then spoon the fish mixture into them and serve with a wedge of lime and fresh coriander to garnish.

Quick tips: For this recipe, you could also use Cod or Bronze Breme instead of the Haddock.

Per Serving: 247 calories; 29g carbs; 24g protein; 6g fiber; 308mg sodium; 51mg cholesterol; 4g fat.

SUMMER SALMON PARCELS

PREP TIME: 15 MINS | COOK TIME: 20 MINS | SERVES: 4

INGREDIENTS:

- 4 6-ounce salmon fillets, without skin
- 2 Cara-Cara oranges, peeled and cut into thin discs
- 2 cups julienne baby marrows
- 1 small onion, sliced
- 2 cups sliced acorn squash,
- Black pepper to taste
- Juice of 1 lemon plus extra to taste
- 1 tbsp. olive oil
- 2 tsp dried thyme
- 4 sprigs fresh thyme
- Tinfoil

DIRECTIONS:

1. Cut out tinfoil parcels about 2 inches longer than the salmon fillets.
2. Preheat the oven to 400°F.
3. Layer the vegetables on the left side of each tinfoil parcel, dividing them equally. Layer them in the following order: acorn squash, baby marrow, onion, orange. Lastly, place the fish fillets on top.
4. Whisk the lemon juice, olive oil and dried thyme together. Pour this equally over each fish fillet, and then top the fillets with a thyme sprig.
5. Close over the parcels, pulling the foil over from the right and sealing the edges well so that the juices can't escape.
6. Place parcels on a baking tray and cook for about 20 minutes until the fish is done.
7. To serve, carefully place the vegetables and fish on a plate attractively and spoon the remaining juices over the top.
8. Enjoy hot.

Per Serving: 309 calories; 18g carbs; 37g protein; 6g fiber; 279mg sodium; 75mg cholesterol; 11g fat.

LEMONY DORADO TRAY BAKE

PREP TIME: 35 MINS | COOK TIME: 15 MINS | SERVES: 2

INGREDIENTS:

- ¼ tsp balsamic vinegar
- ½ tsp minced fresh garlic
- ½ tsp dried oregano
- Juice of ½ lemon
- 2 tsp olive oil, plus extra for baking tray
- 2 7-ounce Dorado steaks
- 1 tbsp. chopped fresh coriander
- 2 lemon wedges

DIRECTIONS:

- Whisk together the vinegar, garlic, dried oregano lemon juice and olive oil. Cover the fish steaks in this marinade and marinade from 15 minutes up to 2 hours.

- Preheat the oven to 400°F.

- Take the fish out of the marinade and place on an oiled baking tray. Cook in the oven for 15 minutes, until done.

- Plate each piece of fish separately, and garnish with fresh coriander and a lemon wedge.

- Serve hot.

Quick tips: To turn this into a full meal, add baby potatoes and baby marrow halves to an oiled tray and bake for 25 minutes. Then go to step 3, placing the fish in the center of the veg and roasting for a further 15 minutes.

Per Serving: 282 calories; 3g carbs; 26g protein; 3g fiber; 101mg sodium; 0mg cholesterol; 18g fat.

LOUISIANA SPICED BLUE CATFISH

PREP TIME: 10 MINS | COOK TIME: 40 MINS | SERVES: 4

INGREDIENTS:

- 8 ounces orange flesh Louisiana sweet potatoes, cut into ½ inch discs
- 8 large cherry tomatoes
- 1 large sweet red pepper, cut into large dice
- 1 cup broccoli florets
- 2 tsp minced fresh garlic
- 1 red onion, roughly chopped
- Black pepper to taste
- 1 tbsp. olive oil, plus extra in a spray bottle
- 4 5-ounce Blue Catfish fillets
- 3 tsp low sodium Cajun seasoning
- 2 lemons, one cut into slices, the other into quarters

DIRECTIONS:

1. Prepare all the veg by oiling a baking tray with olive oil, and toss the cut veg through the oil. Sprinkle 1 tsp of Cajun spice over the veg.

2. Preheat the oven to 400°F.

3. Place the tray of veg in the oven and bake for about 15-20 minutes, until the sweet potatoes are still slightly crunchy. Remove tray from the oven.

4. Add the Catfish fillets to the tray, arranging the veg evenly around them. Place two lemon slices on each fillet and sprinkle over the remaining 2 tsp Cajun spice.

5. Bake the tray for a further 8-10 minutes until the fish is cooked through and flaky.

6. Serve hot as a complete meal, with lemon quarters to garnish.

Per Serving: 282 calories; 18g carbs; 24g protein; 4g fiber; 412mg sodium; 78mg cholesterol; 12g fat.

FRESHWATER FISH CASSEROLE

PREP TIME: 5 MINS | COOK TIME: 15 MIN | SERVES: 2

INGREDIENTS:

- 2 tbsp. fresh lemon juice
- 4 tbsp. olive oil
- Black pepper to taste
- 1 tbsp. finely chopped fresh garlic
- 2 tbsp. chopped flat-leaf parsley
- 1 tbsp. finely chopped thyme
- 2 tbsp. finely chopped white onion
- 1 cup Butternut squash, peeled and largely diced

- 2 cups broccoli florets
- 1 cup zucchini, quartered
- 4 4-ounce tilapia fillets
- 2 tbsp. finely grated pecorino cheese
- 5-ounces fresh rocket
- 2 sprigs parsley to serve

DIRECTIONS:

1. First, make your dressing for the fish by combining 2 tbsp. olive oil with the lemon juice, black pepper, herbs, garlic, and white onion. Set aside.

2. Preheat the oven to 400°F.

3. Next, oil a large casserole dish with olive oil and place the remaining cut veg in it. Drizzle 1 tbsp. oil over them and toss to coat them evenly.

4. Make space for the four fish fillets and pour a small amount of the fish dressing into these spaces. Then place the fillets on top of the dressing and drizzle the remaining dressing over the fish.

5. Bake the casserole in the oven for about 15 minutes until the fish is cooked perfectly and flakes well.

6. To serve, dress the rocket with 2 tsp olive oil, black pepper, and the pecorino cheese.

7. Place the rocket mixture onto plates, with the fish fillets next to it. Spoon the roast veg over the rocket and serve immediately garnished with a sprig of parsley.

Quick tips: Great ideas for serving this dish would be a buttery herbed couscous or crunchy, freshly baked farm-style bread. Brown rice is also a good wholesome option.

Per Serving: 244 calories; 9g carbs; 29g protein; 3g fiber; 208mg sodium; 57mg cholesterol; 13g fat.

JAPANESE YELLOWFIN TUNA

PREP TIME: 10 MINS | COOK TIME: 2 MINS | SERVES: 2

INGREDIENTS:

- 1 tsp olive oil
- ½ tsp minced fresh ginger
- Juice of 1 lime
- 2 tbsp. low sodium soy sauce
- 2 tbsp. wholegrain mustard
- 10-ounces yellowfin tuna, A-grade
- 4 spring onions, finely sliced

DIRECTIONS:

1. Make the marinade first by combining the ginger, lime juice, 1 tbsp. soy sauce and mustard in a bowl. Dunk the steaks into this marinade, coating both sides well.

2. Heat a large non-stick pan and add the olive oil. Sear the tuna in the pan for 1 minute per side. The fish should still be rare on the inside.

3. Serve hot, sliced into ¼-inch slices, and garnished with spring onions and remaining soy sauce on the side.

Quick tips: Another serving suggestion would be to enjoy this with a side of steamed white rice and broccoli florets.

Per Serving: 126 calories; 3g carbs; 18g protein; 1g fiber; 313mg sodium; 0mg cholesterol; 5g fat.

SEAFOOD PAELLA WITH GREEN VEG

PREP TIME: 10 MINS | COOK TIME: 50 MINS | SERVES 6

INGREDIENTS:

- 2 small fresh paprika peppers, diced
- 1 white onion, finely chopped
- 2 tsp minced fresh garlic
- 3 tbsp. chorizo sausage, finely chopped
- 1 tsp dried smoked paprika
- 1 tsp finely chopped fresh rosemary
- 1 tbsp. olive oil
- 1 cup brown rice
- 1 14.5-ounce can chopped tomatoes, low sodium
- 2 cups low sodium chicken stock

- ½ cup water
- 1 tsp dried mixed Italian herbs
- ½ tsp dried chili powder
- ¼ tsp crushed dried saffron
- 12 ounces haddock fillets, cut into cubes
- 8 ounces shrimp, peeled and deveined
- 8 ounces green beans, tops cut and cut in half
- 2 lemons, cut into wedges for serving

DIRECTIONS:

1. Heat the olive oil in a deep bottomed paella pan, then add the onions, fresh paprika, and garlic. Fry for 1 minute, then add the chorizo, smoked paprika and rosemary and fry for a further minute.

2. Add the brown rice and stir, then add the tomatoes, stock, herbs and spices, and water. Cover the pan with a lid and simmer on a low heat for about 40 minutes, or until the rice is al dente.

3. Add in the fish, shrimps and cut green beans and cook for a further 5 minutes, until the fish is cooked through and the flavors have mixed in well.

4. Let the mixture rest for 3 minutes to settle the ingredients, then serve hot with lemon quarters.

Quick tips: Swap out the green beans for any green veg of your choosing. You can also swap the haddock out for Cod if you like.

Per Serving: 266 calories; 35g carbs; 21g protein; 4g fiber; 301mg sodium; 73mg cholesterol; 5g fat.

CAJUN CRUSTED TROUT

PREP TIME: 10 MINS | COOK TIME: 15 MINS | SERVES: 4

INGREDIENTS:

- ¼ tsp chili powder
- 1 tsp treacle sugar
- 1 tsp brown onion powder
- 1 tsp paprika powder
- 2 tsp dried parsley
- 1 tsp dried oregano
- 1 tsp garlic powder
- 1 tsp ground cumin
- Black pepper to taste
- 17 ounces broccoli florets

- 4 6-ounce rainbow trout fillets
- 1 tsp olive oil
- 1 lemon, cut into 4 pieces

DIRECTIONS:

1. Make the crust for the fish by mixing all the dried spices and herbs in a bowl.
2. Lightly oil the fish fillets and then pat the spice crust onto them evenly. Place them on a well-oiled baking tray.
3. Preheat the oven to 425°F and lightly oil a baking tray.
4. Dress the broccoli with a little olive oil and pepper and place on the second oiled baking tray.
5. Bake both trays in the oven at the same time, for about 12-15 minutes, or until the fish and broccoli are superbly cooked. The trout should pull apart effortlessly and have a crisp, dark crust.
6. Serve with lemon quarters for squeezing.

Quick tips: You can easily replace the trout in this recipe with salmon.

Per Serving: 280 calories; 10g carbs; 38g protein; 4g fiber; 227mg sodium; 75mg cholesterol; 11g fat.

CHEESY SHRIMP PASTA

PREP TIME: 5 MINS | COOK TIME: 20 MINS | SERVES: 2

INGREDIENTS:

- 4 ounces penne pasta
- 2 tsp unsalted butter
- 1 tbsp. corn flour
- 2 tbsp. grated mature cheddar
- 1 cup low fat milk
- ¼ cup grated pecorino cheese
- Black pepper to taste
- 1 tbsp. olive oil

- 12 large, pre-cooked frozen shrimp, peeled and deveined
- 1 cup frozen edamame beans
- ½ cup chopped pecans
- ½ tsp mixed Italian herbs

DIRECTIONS:

1. Bring a medium pot of water to a boil, then add the penne and cook at a fast boil for about 8 minutes.

2. Next, make your sauce. Melt the butter in a small pot. Once melted, whisk in the corn flour, making sure there are no lumps. Gradually add the milk, whisking all the time. Bring to a boil and stir until the sauce thickens. Then add black pepper to taste and add the grated cheddar cheese. Add 3 tbsp. parmesan and stir until the cheese melts. Cover to keep warm.

3. At this point, fry up your other ingredients by heating the olive oil in a pan, add the shrimp, edamame beans and pecans and fry for 1 minute. Add the Italian herbs and fry for a further 3 minutes until all the ingredients are hot all the way through.

4. Drain and rinse the pasta in hot water, then throw it into the cheesy sauce. Stir well.

5. Spoon the pasta into the serving bowls and cascade the shrimp mixture over the top to serve.

6. Enjoy hot.

Quick tips: You can store this in the fridge for up to 3 days.

Per Serving: 673 calories; 64g carbs; 31g protein; 6g fiber; 653mg sodium; 0mg cholesterol; 34g fat.

LEMONY COD WITH ROAST VEG

PREP TIME 15 MINS | COOK TIME 25 MINS | SERVES: 4

INGREDIENTS:

- 2 cups brown rice
- 2 large orange sweet potatoes, cut into cubes
- 3 cups broccoli florets
- 8 cherry tomatoes
- 3 tbsp. olive oil
- Black pepper to taste
- ½ cup dry white wine
- ¼ chives, finely chopped, plus extra for garnish
- 2 tsp minced fresh garlic

- 1 tbsp. ginger finely chopped
- 2 lemons, sliced
- 4 4-ounce Cod fillets.

DIRECTIONS:

1. Place the brown rice in a medium pot. Add water so that it covers the rice by about two fingers. Bring to a boil and cook until done and all the liquid has been absorbed.

2. Preheat the oven to 400°F, oil a baking tray.

3. Place the veg onto the baking tray, drizzle with olive and pepper to taste, and then bake for about 25 minutes, until crisp golden edges form on the veg. Remove from the oven just before serving.

4. Heat 1 tbsp. olive oil in a pan and sear the cod fillets for about 5 minutes. Remove from the pan and turn off the heat for now.

5. Mix together 1 tbsp. olive oil, the ginger, garlic and lemon slices. Then turn the heat back on and throw them in the pan. Sauté them until the lemons gain good color. Add the wine and chives and reduce for 3 minutes to form a sauce. Add the fish and rice to the pan and cook until the rice has absorbed all the liquid and the fish is cooked through.

6. Serve by spooning the rice onto the plates with some of the sauce, then place the cod on top. Place the roast veg next to the fish and rice and garnish with a sprinkling of chopped chives.

7. Enjoy hot.

Per Serving: 450 calories; 53g carbs; 32g protein; 9g fiber; 187mg sodium; 62mg cholesterol; 13g fat.

RED MEAT

FAMILY MEATLOAF

PREP TIME: 20 MINS | COOK TIME: 50 MINS | SERVES: 8

INGREDIENTS:

- ½ cup cous-cous
- 1 cup water
- 2 tbsp. finely chopped garlic
- 2 small paprika pepper, diced
- 1 medium red onion, diced
- 1 tsp mixed dried herbs
- 2 tbsp. olive oil, plus extra in a spray bottle
- ¼ cup plus 2 tbsp. barbeque sauce

- 1 tbsp. balsamic vinegar
- Black pepper to taste
- 2 large egg whites
- 17.5 ounces lean beef mince

DIRECTIONS:

1. Place the cous-cous in a bowl. Boil the water and pour over the cous-cous. Cover, and leave to absorb the water for about 15-20 minutes.

2. Make your flavor base by heating olive oil in pan, then add the onion, paprika, garlic, and herbs and fry off for about 6 minutes. Set aside to cool.

3. Preheat the oven to 350°F.

4. Drain the cous-cous and then mix it in with the onion mixture. Add the barbeque sauce and balsamic vinegar and mix well. Season with black pepper to taste.

5. Mix in the egg whites, and finally stir in the raw mince.

6. Line a baking tray with foil, oil it, and shape the mince mixture into one medium-sized loaf. Bake for about 40 minutes or until cooked through.

7. In the last 5 minutes of cooking, brush the last 2 tbsp. of barbeque sauce over the top of the loaf, and bake off to caramelize.

8. Remove from the oven and let rest for 10 minutes.

9. Serve hot and sliced.

Per Serving: 162 calories; 16g carbs; 15g protein; 3g fiber; 322mg sodium; 35mg cholesterol; 4g fat

PEPPERED FILET WITH RED WINE SAUCE

PREP TIME: 7 MINS | COOK TIME: 13 MINS | SERVES: 4

INGREDIENTS:

- 1 cup low sodium beef stock
- ¼ cup red wine
- ¼ cup finely chopped red onion
- ½ tsp finely chopped rosemary, plus 4 sprigs to garnish
- 1 tbsp. unsalted butter
- 1 tsp olive oil, plus extra in a spray bottle
- Black pepper to taste
- 4 6-ounce filet mignons

- 1 tsp green peppercorns
- 1 tsp red peppercorns
- ½ tsp black peppercorn
- ½ tsp white peppercorns

DIRECTIONS:

1. First, make the sauce. Heat 1 tsp of the oil in a small pot, add the onion and rosemary and fry off for about 2 minutes. Then add the wine and allow to reduce off almost completely. Add the stock and simmer to reduce by half. Remove from the heat and whisk in the butter and black pepper to taste. Cover to keep warm.

2. Crush up all the peppercorns together. Place the filets on a plate and then crust them evenly on all sides with the peppercorns. Press the peppercorns into the meat to make sure it sticks.

3. Spray a non-stick pan with olive oil and heat. Cook the steaks at medium heat for about 4 minutes a side to get a medium-rare finish.

4. Serve hot with a tbsp. of the sauce drizzled over the tops and a sprig of rosemary to garnish.

Per Serving: 315 calories; 2g carbs; 34g protein; 0g fiber; 123mg sodium; 104gm cholesterol; 14g fat.

CHINESE-STYLE BEEF STIR-FRY

PREP TIME: 10 MINS | COOK TIME: 12 MINS | SERVES: 2

INGREDIENTS:

- 8 ounces beef sirloin, sliced into strips
- 2 tsp canola oil
- ¾ cup orange juice
- 1 tsp brown sugar
- 1 tbsp. apple cider vinegar
- 1 tsp peanut oil
- 1 tbsp. low sodium soy sauce
- 2 tbsp. corn flour

- ¼ tsp Chines 5-spice mix
- 1 tsp chili flakes
- 3 cups mixed veg, cut stir fry style, frozen
- 2 tsp minced fresh ginger
- 3 tsp finely chopped garlic

DIRECTIONS:

1. In a pan or a wok, fry the beef off in 1 tsp of hot oil. Fry for about 3-4 minutes, and set aside, covered to stay warm.

2. Make the sauce by combining the orange juice, sugar, vinegar, peanut oil, soy sauce, Chinese 5-spice, chili, and corn flour. Whisk well to incorporate the flour without any lumps.

3. Add the remaining oil to the wok and fry the garlic and ginger off for 1 minute. Add the veg mix and cook until thawed. Add in the sauce and cook for 2 minutes. Lastly, add the beef and cook until heated through and the sauce is thick and shiny.

4. Serve hot. Yum.

Quick tips: This recipe is great served with steamed white rice.

Per Serving: 321 calories; 22g carbs; 28g protein; 4g fiber; 376mg sodium; 65mg cholesterol; 3g fat.

MEATBALLS IN TOMATO SAUCE

PREP TIME: 15 MINS | COOK TIME: 15 MINS | SERVE 2-3

INGREDIENTS:

- 2 tbsp. olive oil, plus extra
- 1 small white onion finely chopped
- 6 ounces lean beef mince
- 2 ounces lean minced chicken
- 1 large egg
- ½ cup rolled oats
- 2 tbsp. low fat milk
- 2 tbsp. fresh parsley, finely chopped, plus extra to serve
- 2 tbsp. finely chopped thyme

- Black pepper to taste
- 1 tbsp. finely chopped garlic
- 1 14-ounce can chopped tomatoes
- ¼ tsp chili flakes
- 3 ounces grated cheddar cheese

DIRECTIONS:

1. Mix the meatball ingredients in a bowl: onion, beef mince, chicken mince, egg, oats, milk, herbs, and black pepper. Roll out 8 meatballs from this mixture.

2. Heat 1 tbsp. of the olive oil in a medium-sized deep pan. Fry off the meatballs on medium heat for 6-7 minutes, turning every so often to brown all the sides.

3. Remove the meatballs from the pan and place on a plate.

4. Add the remaining oil, and then add the garlic and chili flakes. Fry for one minute before adding the tomatoes and cook for 2 minutes to reduce slightly.

5. Put the meatballs back in the pan with the tomato sauce. Cover with a lid and simmer on low heat for about minutes until the meatballs are heated through and the sauce thickened.

6. Preheat the grill while this is cooking.

7. Sprinkle over the grated cheese and place the pan under the grill for 2 minutes to brown the cheese.

8. Serve hot with chopped parsley sprinkled over the top.

Quick tips: This can be stored in the fridge for up to 3 days. A delicious serving suggestion would be to serve this meal with steaming baby marrow noodles.

Per Serving: 516 calories; 29g carbs; 41g protein; 5g fiber; 812mg sodium; 0mg cholesterol; 26g fat.

SIRLOIN COOKED WITH ASIAN RUB

PREP TIME: 10 MINS | COOK TIME 8 MINS | SERVES: 8

INGREDIENTS:

Sauce:
- 2 tsp red curry paste
- 1 ½ tsp rice vinegar
- 1 tsp minced garlic
- 2 tsp low sodium soy sauce
- 2 tsp finely chopped ginger
- ¼ cup smooth low sodium peanut butter
- 3 tbsp. brewed cold coffee
- 3 tbsp. coconut milk

Rub:
- 1 tsp red curry paste
- ½ tsp ground ginger
- ½ garlic powder
- Black pepper to taste

Steaks:
- Olive oil in a spray bottle
- 8 3-ounce sirloin steaks, 1 inch thick
- Chopped fresh mint to serve

DIRECTIONS:

1. Make the sauce first: Blend the 2 tsp curry paste, vinegar, garlic, soy sauce, ginger, peanut butter, coffee, and coconut milk until the sauce is thick and creamy. Set aside.

2. Preheat and oil a griddle pan.

3. Stir the rub ingredients together: 1 tsp curry paste, ginger, garlic powder, and black pepper. Rub this onto the sirloins, evenly distributing it across the meat.

4. Cook the steaks on a hot griddle pan for about 3 minutes a side for a medium-rare finish.

5. Remove from the heat and let the steaks rest for 3 minutes.

6. To serve: Slice the steaks and place on a plate with the peanut sauce in small ramekins. Sprinkle chopped mint over the steak and enjoy hot.

Quick tips: Serve leftover peanut sauce with raw vegetables as a delicious snack.

Per Serving: 387 calories; 10g carbs; 27g protein; 1g fiber; 312mg sodium; 80mg cholesterol; 19g fat.

SPICY ENCHILADA BAKE

PREP TIME: 15 MINS | COOK TIME: 20 MINS | SERVES 3-4

INGREDIENTS:

- ½ tsp olive oil, plus extra in a spray bottle
- 8 ounces lean beef mince
- 1 small white onion, finely chopped
- 2 tsp chili powder
- ¾ tsp ground cumin
- ¼ tsp ground paprika
- 4 tbsp. tomato paste
- 1 cup cooked cannellini beans, drained

- ½ cup water
- 15 ounces cooked butternut squash, pureed
- ½ cup low sodium beef stock
- 4 soft tortilla wraps
- 1/3 cup grated Cantal cheese
- ½ cup low fat yogurt, to serve
- Sprig of parsley to garnish

DIRECTIONS:

1. Start by heating the oil in a medium pan and adding in the onions. Fry off for 1 minute, then add in the beef mince and fry for about 8 minutes. Then add in 1 tsp chili powder, ¼ tsp cumin, ¼ tsp paprika powder and 2 tbsp. tomato paste. Stir to mix in, then add the beans and water. Cook for about 2 minutes and set aside.

2. Preheat the oven to 350°F.

3. Next make the sauce by heating up the butternut puree with the remaining spices and tomato paste. Then add the beef stock and simmer on low until a smooth sauce is formed.

4. Oil a deep baking dish and then pour in ½ cup of the sauce and spread evenly over the bottom.

5. Divide the beef mixture evenly amongst the wraps, then roll them up tightly and place snugly in the baking dish.

6. Cover the wraps evenly with the remaining sauce, add the grated cheese over the top and then bake for 20-25 minutes.

7. Serve with a spoonful of yogurt over the top, and a sprig of parsley to garnish.

8. Enjoy hot!

Quick tips: Make this a vegetarian dish by replacing the mince with ½ cup extra beans, and ½ cup sliced, cooked mushrooms.

Per Serving: 566 calories; 66g carbs; 36g protein; 12g fiber; 681mg sodium; 0mg cholesterol; 18g fat.

MEDITERRANEAN LEG OF LAMB

PREP TIME: 60 MINS | COOK TIME: 25 MINS | SERVES: 6

INGREDIENTS:

- 28-ounce leg of lamb, fat trimmed off, butterflied
- ½ cup pomegranate juice
- ½ cup dry sherry
- 1 tsp dried basil
- 1 tsp ground cumin
- 3 tbsp. finely chopped garlic
- ½ tsp dried chili
- Olive oil in a spray bottle
- Black pepper to taste
- ½ fresh pomegranate jewels to garnish

DIRECTIONS:

1. Place the leg of lamb in a deep Tupperware that can seal.

2. Make up the marinade by mixing the pomegranate juice, sherry, basil, cumin, garlic, and chili together. Pour the marinade over the lamb, making sure it covers the meat.

3. Let marinade in the fridge for 1 hour. Stir occasionally to achieve an even marinade.

4. Remove the lamb from the oven and drain. The surface of the meat should be juicy but not sopping. Season with black pepper to taste.

5. Turn on the grill to heat up.

6. Oil a roasting rack and place the lamb on it. Place under the grill with an oven tray underneath it to catch the juices.

7. Roast for about 20 minutes for a medium-rare leg of lamb.

8. Let the meat rest for 5 minutes, then carve into serving slices, plate, and garnish with fresh pomegranate jewels.

9. Enjoy hot.

Quick tips: You can use the drippings in the baking tray to make a delicious jus for the meat. Simply take the juices from the pan, place them in a small pot and simmer on low until reduced to a thick jus. Serve drizzled over the meat.

Per Serving: 273 calories; 0g carbs; 31g protein; 0g fiber; 219mg sodium; 91mg cholesterol; 15g fat.

PARMESAN CRUSTED PORK

PREP TIME: 10 MINS | COOK TIME: 50 MINS | SERVES: 4

INGREDIENTS:

- ¼ cup cornflakes, ground to breadcrumb size
- ¼ cup parmesan cheese, finely grated
- 1 tsp fresh thyme, finely chopped
- 2 tsp finely chopped garlic
- Black pepper to taste

- 16-ounce pork tenderloin
- Olive oil in a spray bottle
- 1 small red onion, sliced into thin rounds
- 4 sprigs fresh thyme to garnish

DIRECTIONS:

1. Make your crumb mixture by mixing the cornflakes, parmesan, thyme, garlic, and black pepper in a shallow dish.

2. Roll the tenderloin in the crumbs, coating thickly and evenly on all sides.

3. Preheat the oven to 375°F.

4. Lightly oil a baking tray with olive oil, then lay the onion down on the tray. Place the crumbed tenderloin on top of the onions and bake in the oven for about 45-50 minutes.

5. Remove from the oven and then allow the tenderloin to rest for 10 minutes, covered.

6. Slice, and serve hot, garnished with a sprig of thyme.

Quick tips: You can replace the cornflakes with Panko breadcrumbs if you wish, or even ground almond flour for a gluten-free option.

Per Serving: 196 calories; 6g carbs; 28g protein; 1g fiber; 316mg sodium; 72mg cholesterol; 6g fat.

SWEET & SOUR PORK CHOPS

PREP TIME: 10 MINUTES | COOK TIME: 70 MINS | SERVES: 4

INGREDIENTS:

Sweet and Sour Cabbage:
- 1 tbsp. olive oil
- 1 medium red onion, sliced
- 2 rashers low sodium back bacon, cut into cubes
- ½ medium sized white cabbage, sliced
- ¼ cup white grape vinegar
- 3 tbsp. golden syrup
- ¼ cup water
- 2 crisp green apples, peeled and diced

- Black pepper to taste

Pork Chops:
- Olive oil in a spray bottle
- 4 4-ounce pork chops, fat removed
- Black pepper to taste

DIRECTIONS:

1. Heat the oil in a pan, add the onion and fry for 1 minute. Then add the bacon pieces and cook until crispy and browned. Add ⅓ of the cabbage, and sprinkle over ⅓ of the vinegar. Repeat this process until the cabbage and vinegar are all incorporated.

2. Then add the syrup, water, apples, and black pepper and reduce the heat. Leave to simmer on low for about 1 hour.

3. 10 minutes before the cabbage is ready, heat and oil a non-stick pan.

4. Place the pork chops in the pan and fry until golden brown on each side, about 3 minutes a side. While cooking, add black pepper to taste. Set aside covered to keep warm.

5. Transfer the cabbage mixture to the hot chops pan and stir well on high for 3 minutes.

6. To serve, use a slotted spoon. To avoid getting juices on the plate, spoon the cabbage mixture neatly onto the center of the plate and place the hot chops on top.

7. Enjoy.

Per Serving: 356 calories; 39g carbs; 29g protein; 6g fiber; 377mg sodium; 66mg cholesterol; 10g fat.

MIDDLE AMERICAN PORK AND BEANS

PREP TIME: 75 MINS | COOK TIME 25 MINS | SERVES: 4

INGREDIENTS:

- 16-ounce pork tenderloin

Marinade
- 1 tsp chili flakes
- 1 tsp dried basil
- 1 tsp dried cumin
- ½ tsp paprika
- ¼ cup grapefruit juice
- 1 lime, zested and juiced
- 2 tbsp. olive oil

Beans
- 1 tbsp. canola oil
- 1 tbsp. ground cumin
- 2 tsp dried basil
- 2 spring onions, finely chopped
- 2 small fresh paprika peppers
- 1 large oxheart tomato, diced
- 15 ounces cooked red kidney beans, drained
- ½ cup low sodium beef stock
- ¼ cup chopped fresh parsley
- 2 tbsp. finely chopped fresh coriander

DIRECTIONS:

1. Make the marinade first by incorporating all the marinade ingredients, except 1 tbsp. oil, together in a deep Tupperware. Place the pork in the Tupperware, making sure the marinade covers the top. Cover with Tupperware lid.

2. Marinade the pork in the fridge for up to 1 hour.

3. To make the beans, heat the oil in a medium pan. Add the spring onions and dried spices, and herbs and fry for about 2 minutes. Add the paprika and cook for a further 4 minutes, until the veg is soft. Then add the tomatoes, beans, and stock.

4. Turn the heat down on the beans, cover, and leave to simmer for about 5 minutes. In the last minute, add all the parsley except 2 tbsp.

5. In the meantime, cook the pork tenderloin. Take the pork out of the marinade, but do not discard the marinade. Slice the pork into thin discs.

6. Heat the remaining 1 tbsp. oil in a pan, add the pork to the pan and fry for 5 minutes. Turn the pork over, and then add the marinade into the pan, and cook the tenderloins thoroughly in the sauce for about 5-7 minutes.

7. Plate the beans up and lay the pork over the top attractively. Garnish with the chopped herbs and serve hot.

Quick tips: Serve this dish with hearty brown rice or 2 slices of toasted seed bread.

Per Serving: 310 calories; 25g carbs; 31g protein; 6g fiber; 228mg sodium; 45mg cholesterol; 11g fat.

PORK POKE BOWL

PREP TIME: 10 MINS | COOK TIME: 10 MINS | SERVES: 2

INGREDIENTS:

- 1 tsp olive oil
- 1 large red pepper, sliced
- 1 small red onion, sliced
- ½ tsp smoked paprika
- ¼ tsp cayenne pepper
- 1 tsp minced garlic
- 1 tbsp. low sodium soy sauce
- 2 tbsp. water
- 1 tbsp. maple syrup

- ¾ cup cooked and drained brown and wild rice
- 6 ounces pulled roast pork loin
- 1 ½ cups cherry tomatoes, halved
- ¼ cucumber, finely sliced into rounds
- 1 avocado, sliced
- Fresh coriander to garnish.

DIRECTIONS:

1. Heat the oil in a medium pan. Add in the onions, red pepper, paprika, cayenne pepper, and garlic and fry off for 3-4 minutes, until the veg are cooked but still slightly crispy.

2. Make a soy glaze by combining the soy sauce, water, and maple syrup in a small bowl.

3. To assemble, use deep round bowls. Spoon the rice into half the bowl, then place the pulled pork on the other. Lay the onion and pepper mixture in the middle of the two, then arrange the fresh veg appealingly on either side of the peppers. Fan the sliced avocado out in the center and drizzle the soy glaze over the whole bowl.

4. Garnish with fresh coriander and enjoy.

Quick tips: You can easily replace the rice in this dish with cooked quinoa. Instead of using cooked pulled pork, you could also use 6 ounces pork mince, which you would fry up in a tbsp. olive oil, using the same spices you use on the onion and red peppers.

Per Serving: 751 calories; 72g carbs; 30g protein; 16g fiber; 255mg sodium; 0mg cholesterol; 40g fat.

MUSTARDY PORK CHOPS

PREP TIME: 5 MINS | COOK TIME: 10 MINS | SERVES: 4

INGREDIENTS:

- ½ cup low sodium chicken stock
- 2 tsp corn flour
- 1 tsp olive oil
- Black pepper to taste
- 6 4-ounce pork chops
- 1 tbsp. unsalted butter
- 2 tbsp. white onion, finely chopped

- ½ cup low fat milk
- 1 tbsp. wholegrain mustard
- 1 tbsp. chopped fresh parsley
- 1 tbsp. chopped fresh tarragon

DIRECTIONS:

1. Combine the stock and corn flour in a bowl using a whisk. Make sure there are no lumps in the mixture.

2. Heat the olive oil in a pan, season the chops with black pepper and then fry them off in the pan for 3 minutes a side. Set aside to rest.

3. Then start making the sauce. Melt the butter in a large saucepan, add in the onion and sauté' for 2 minutes. Add the milk and mustard to the stock mixture and whisk again to ensure a smooth liquid. Pour this mixture into the pan with the onions and bring to a boil.

4. Arrange the chops in the boiling sauce, adding any juices to the sauce. Cook for 1 minute, turning at least twice in that time.

5. Arrange 1 ½ pork chops on each plate, drizzle the sauce over them, and garnish with the chopped fresh herbs.

Per Serving: 207 calories; 3g carbs; 25g protein; 0g fiber; 323mg sodium; 73g cholesterol; 10g fat.

FANCY PORK FAJITAS

PREP TIME: 15 MINS | COOK TIME: 25 MINS | SERVES: 4

INGREDIENTS:

- 16 ounces pork loin, cut into slices
- 1 tbsp. olive oil
- 2 spring onions, cut into semi-thick slices at an angle
- 5 fresh paprika peppers sliced
- 2 tbsp. garlic finely chopped
- 1 tsp smoked paprika
- 1 tsp cumin
- ½ minced fresh chili
- Black pepper to taste
- 4 soft flour wraps
- 1 avocado, peeled and cut into slices
- 1 lemon, cut into quarters
- Fresh coriander to serve

DIRECTIONS:

1. First, fry off the pork by heating the oil in a medium pan and adding the pork. Fry for about 5-10 minutes until the pork is well browned and cooked all the way through.

2. Remove the pork from the pan and set aside.

3. Add the spring onions, paprika, garlic, chili, dried spices, and black pepper to the pan and fry for about 5 minutes until the veg is cooked. Then add the pork back into the pan, and fry for another minute.

4. Heat a non-stick pan, and lightly warm up and toast the wraps in the pan one by one.

5. To serve, spoon the pork mixture into the wraps, add the avocado, fanned out on top. Squeeze over some lemon juice and garnish with fresh coriander.

Per Serving: 366 calories; 29g carbs; 29g protein; 8g fiber; 203mg sodium; 67mg cholesterol; 16g fat.

STEWS & SOUPS

SPICY CHICKEN AND CORN SOUP

PREP TIME: 10 MINS | COOK TIME: 45 MINS | SERVES: 8

INGREDIENTS:

- 24 ounces chicken breast meat, cut into medium pieces
- 1 tbsp. olive oil
- 1 red onion, diced
- 2 tbsp. finely chopped garlic
- 1 sweet red pepper, diced
- 1 large chili, deseeded and finely chopped
- Black pepper to taste

- 3 cups low sodium chicken stock
- 3 cups water
- 14.5 ounce can chopped tomatoes
- 1 cup fresh corn kernels, cut off the cob
- 1 cup broccoli florets
- 2 tbsp. fresh coriander chopped, plus extra to serve
- 2 limes, cut into quarters
- Olive oil in a spray bottle
- 3 6-inch hard shell corn tortillas, cut into large strips

DIRECTIONS:

1. Heat the olive oil in a large pot, then fry off half the chicken pieces until light brown. Remove from the pot and fry off the second half. Add the rest of the chicken back into the pot.

2. Then add in the onions, garlic, red pepper, chili, and black pepper. Fry for about 5 minutes or until the onion is almost cooked.

3. Preheat the oven to 400°F.

4. Add in the chicken stock and stir well to deglaze any pieces on the bottom of the pan. Pour in the water and the chopped tomatoes. Bring to a boil.

5. Lower the heat, and then simmer the soup uncovered for about 35 minutes until the chicken is cooked through.

6. Spray the tortilla strips with a little olive oil, then bake off in the oven for about 5-10 minutes, until golden and crisp. Set aside to cool.

7. 5 minutes before the soup is done, add in the corn and broccoli florets, as well as 2 tbsp. chopped coriander.

8. Spoon into serving bowls, place tortilla strips over the side and sprinkle over some chopped coriander to garnish. Serve hot with a lime quarter on the side.

Per Serving: 194 calories; 16g carbs; 19g protein; 3g fiber; 387mg sodium; 66mg cholesterol; 10g fat.

VICHYSSOISE SOUP WITH A TWIST

PREP TIME: 15 MINS | COOK TIME: 30 MINS | SERVES: 4

INGREDIENTS:

- 1 white onion, finely chopped
- 2 tbsp. minced garlic
- 1 tsp ground paprika
- 1 tbsp. olive oil
- 8 ounces Bellerose potatoes, washed and diced
- 8 ounces orange flesh sweet potato, washed and diced
- 2 cups cauliflower florets

- 3 cups low sodium chicken stock
- 1 cup coconut milk
- Black pepper to taste
- ¼ cup finely chopped fresh parsley

DIRECTIONS:

1. Start by frying the onion, garlic, and paprika off in the olive oil, in a large pot, for about 2 minutes until the onion is translucent.

2. Add in the potatoes, sweet potatoes, and cauliflower. Fry for 2 minutes, then pour in the chicken stock. Bring to a boil and cook for about 10 minutes, or until the potatoes are soft.

3. Place this mixture in a high-powered blender, then blend until completely smooth.

4. Return this to the pot, then add in the coconut milk and black pepper to taste.

5. Spoon into the serving bowls and top with parsley.

6. Enjoy hot.

Quick tips: To make this soup vegetarian, use a vegetable-based stock instead of the chicken stock. Serve this soup with a big salad, some cooked green veg, and rice for a complete meal.

Per Serving: 181 calories; 33g carbs; 6g protein; 6g fiber; 182mg fiber; 1mg cholesterol; 4g fat.

CHICKEN MINESTRONE

PREP TIME: 5 MINS | COOK TIME: 55 MINS | SERVES: 8

INGREDIENTS:

- 20 ounces chicken and sage sausage, outer casing removed
- 1 tbsp. olive oil
- 2 tbsp. finely chopped garlic
- 1 tsp dried mixed Italian herbs
- 2 tbsp. fresh finely chopped oregano
- 2 shallots, diced
- 2 sweet carrots, peeled and diced
- 2 stalks celery, diced
- 5 cups low sodium chicken stock
- 1 14.5-ounce can chopped tomatoes
- 2 cups water
- ½ tsp dried chili flakes
- 1 bay leaf
- ½ cup baby marrow, diced
- 4 cups spinach, washed and destemmed
- 1 15-ounce can of cannellini beans, drained
- ¼ cup fresh basil, finely chopped, plus 8 sprigs to garnish
- ½ cup fresh parsley finely chopped

DIRECTIONS:

1. Cut the sausage into pieces. Then heat the olive oil in a large deep pot and add in the sausage. Fry off for 6 minutes.

2. After 6 minutes, add in the garlic, herbs, shallots, carrot, and celery. Cook for about 5 minutes or until the shallots are translucent.

3. Pour in the stock, add the canned tomatoes, water, chili flakes, and bay leaf. Bring soup to a boil and cook on medium heat for 30 minutes.

4. Add the baby marrow, spinach, beans, and fresh chopped herbs. Stir in and cook for a further 15 minutes until the vegetables are all soft.

5. Scoop out the bay leaf and discard.

6. Serve hot spooned into bowls with a sprig of basil to garnish.

Per Serving: 205 calories; 19g carbs; 16g protein; 5g fiber; 659mg sodium; 21mg cholesterol; 8g fat.

PUMPKIN AND COCONUT SOUP

PREP TIME: 10 MINS | COOK TIME: 15 MINS | SERVES: 2

INGREDIENTS:

- 2 tbsp. Coconut oil
- 1 tbsp. tomato paste
- ½ tsp ground cumin
- ¼ tsp ground ginger
- ¼ tsp ground cinnamon
- 1 tbsp. chili paste
- 4 cups low sodium vegetable stock

- 1 15-ounce can of coconut milk
- 10 ounces frozen cooked pumpkin
- Low fat yogurt to garnish
- Chili oil, to garnish

DIRECTIONS:

1. Melt the coconut oil on medium heat in a large pot.

2. Add in the tomato paste, spices, and chili paste and fry for 1 minute.

3. Then pour in the stock and coconut milk and stir well to mix. Bring to a boil.

4. Add the pumpkin and cook for about 14 minutes until the pumpkin is fully heated through and soft.

5. Transfer soup to a blender, and blend on high until completely smooth.

6. Return to the pot, reheat, and then serve hot with a spoonful of yogurt and a drizzle of chili oil.

Quick tips: You can substitute the pumpkin for butternut if you'd like, as well as using chicken stock instead of vegetable.

Per Serving: 630 calories; 35g carbs; 17g protein; 3g fiber; 290mg sodium; 0mg cholesterol; 54g fat.

WARMING MEATY SOUP

PREP TIME: 10 MINS | COOK TIME: 30 MINS | SERVES: 8

INGREDIENTS:

- 1 tbsp. olive oil
- 24 ounces ground beef chuck
- 2 cups diced red onion
- 2 sweet carrots, diced
- 2 stalks celery, diced
- 2 medium celeriac roots, diced
- 1 tbsp. fresh finely chopped thyme
- 2 cups uncooked barley

- 5 cups low sodium beef stock
- 2 cups water
- 1 14.5-ounce can chopped tomatoes
- Black pepper to taste
- 1 bay leaf

DIRECTIONS:

1. Heat the oil in a large pot, add the ground beef and cook for about 5 minutes.
2. Add the onion, carrots, celery, celeriac, and thyme to the pot and fry for a further 5 minutes until the onion is soft.
3. Add in the barley and stir to mix well.
4. Pour in the stock, water, and chopped tomatoes. Add the bay leaf and season to taste with black pepper.
5. Bring to a boil and cook for about 20 minutes, until the barley and vegetables are soft.
6. Serve hot and enjoy.

Per Serving: 272 calories; 28g carbs; 24g protein; 5g fiber; 395mg sodium; 53mg cholesterol; 7g fat.

SPICY NORTH AFRICAN SOUP

PREP TIME: 10 MINS | COOK TIME: 31 MINS | SERVES: 4

INGREDIENTS:

- 1 tbsp. olive oil
- 2 small red onions, diced
- 1 tbsp. minced garlic
- ¾ cup finely chopped celery
- 1 sweet red pepper, diced
- ½ tsp chili powder
- ½ tsp cinnamon
- ½ tsp ground cumin
- ½ tsp ground coriander
- ½ tsp ground ginger
- ½ tsp smoked paprika
- ½ tsp ground star anise
- 2 tbsp. tomato paste
- 1 cup brown lentils
- 4 cups low sodium chicken stock
- ¼ cup low fat yogurt to serve

DIRECTIONS:

1. Heat olive oil in a large pot, then add the onion, celery, red pepper, and fry for 3 minutes. Then add in all the dried ground spices and fry for 1 minute.

2. Add in the tomato paste and stir. Fry for a further 2 minutes.

3. Rinse the lentils in cold water, drain off the water and then add them to the pot. Pour in the stock and then bring to a boil.

4. Cook for about 25 minutes on medium heat or until the lentils are soft.

5. Serve hot with a dollop of yogurt on top to garnish.

Quick tips: You can use any type of lentil for this soup. Green lentils are a particularly delicious option. Store this soup in the fridge for up to 3 days.

Per Serving: 230 calories; 38g carbs; 13g protein; 7g fiber; 21mg sodium; 0mg cholesterol; 4g fat.

NEW ENGLAND CLAM CHOWDER

PREP TIME: 10 MINS | COOK TIME: 35 MINS | SERVES: 8

INGREDIENTS:

- ½ cup pancetta, cut into cubes
- 1 tsp olive oil
- 8 ounces potato, washed and diced
- 2 ¼ cups water
- 1 tbsp. unsalted butter
- 2 shallots, diced
- ½ tsp fresh thyme, finely chopped, extra sprigs to serve
- Black pepper to taste
- 1 ¾ cups low sodium chicken stock
- 2 cups low fat milk
- 2 tbsp. corn flour
- 1 cup clams, chopped, with juices

DIRECTIONS:

1. Heat the olive oil in a large pot and fry the pancetta cubes until crispy and brown, about 5 minutes. Set aside to cool.

2. Meanwhile, bring 2 cups of water to a boil in a separate pot, and boil the potato until cooked, about 15 minutes.

3. Add the butter to the pancetta pot, turn the heat back on, and add the shallots, thyme, and black pepper. Fry until the shallots are translucent, about 3 minutes.

4. Add the pancetta back into the pot along with the potatoes and their water, the stock, and the milk. Bring to a boil and then cook on medium heat for 10 minutes.

5. Whisk the corn flour into the remaining ¼ cup water, and then add it into the soup. Whisk well to prevent lumps forming.

6. Add in the clams and their juices, bring back to a boil and remove from heat.

7. Serve hot with a sprig of thyme to garnish.

Per Serving: 120 calories; 12g carbs; 9g protein; 0.7g fiber; 424mg sodium; 19mg cholesterol; 4g fat.

SPICY BEEF CHILI

PREP TIME: 10 MINS | COOK TIME: 30 MINS | SERVES: 6

INGREDIENTS:

- 1 red onion, diced
- 2 medium sweet fresh paprika peppers
- 2 tbsp. finely chopped garlic
- 1 tbsp. canola oil
- 2 tbsp. fresh coriander, finely chopped, plus extra sprigs to garnish

- 20 ounces lean beef mince
- ½ tsp smoked paprika
- ½ cup chipotle chilies, with adobo, minced
- 2 tbsp. dried chili powder
- 28-ounce can chopped tomatoes
- 2 15-ounce cans black beans, drained

DIRECTIONS:

1. Fry the onion and paprika peppers in hot oil in a medium pot for about 3 minutes. Then add in the garlic and fresh coriander and fry for another minute.

2. Add the beef mince and stir well. Then add in the paprika and two different types of chili. Cook for about 6 minutes until the mince is no longer pink.

3. Add in the tomatoes and bring to a low simmer. Cook for a further 15 minutes until the mince is cooked, and the flavors have blended beautifully. Five minutes before turning the heat off, add the black beans, and cook until heated through.

4. Serve hot, garnished with fresh coriander.

Quick tips: You can also serve this with 2 tbsp. grated cheddar cheese and 1 tbsp. low fat sour cream for an authentic chili feel.

Per Serving: 288 calories; 24g carbs; 28g protein; 7g fiber; 428mg sodium; 67mg cholesterol; 8g fat.

MASALA CHICKPEAS

PREP TIME: 10 MINS | COOK TIME: 25 MINS | SERVES: 4

INGREDIENTS:

- 1 ½ tsp Garam masala powder
- 1 tsp smoked paprika
- 1 tsp jeera powder
- 1 tsp ground coriander
- 1 tsp turmeric powder
- ¼ tsp cayenne pepper
- 1 tbsp. canola oil
- ½ tsp black mustard seeds
- 2 tbsp. jeera seeds
- 1 white onion, diced
- 4 tbsp. finely chopped garlic
- 1 large sweet red pepper, diced
- 2 rosa tomatoes, roughly chopped
- ½ cup broccoli florets
- 1 medium carrot, peeled and cut into cubes
- 2 cups water
- 30 ounces cooked chickpeas, rinsed and drained
- 1 tbsp. tomato paste
- 10 ounces frozen kale, thawed
- Black pepper to taste
- 2 tbsp. finely chopped fresh coriander, plus extra to garnish

DIRECTIONS:

1. In a small bowl, make the spice blend by mixing all the dried spices, except for the jeera seeds and mustard seeds. Set aside.

2. Heat the oil in a medium pot, then add in the mustard seeds and jeera seeds. Cook for 10 seconds before adding in the onion and garlic. Fry for 3 minutes.

3. Add in the following vegetables: red pepper, tomatoes, broccoli, and carrots. Then cook the mixture on medium heat for about 6 minutes.

4. Pour in two cups of water, then add the chickpeas, tomato paste, kale, and black pepper to taste. Bring to a slow boil and cook for about 15-20 minutes, or until the vegetables are cooked through, and the stew smells aromatic.

5. Serve hot, with a sprinkling of freshly chopped coriander.

Per Serving: 309 calories; 50g carbs; 15g protein; 14g fiber; 134mg sodium; 0mg cholesterol; 7g fat.

NEW YORK CHOWDER

PREP TIME: 10 MINS | COOK TIME: 35 MINS | SERVES: 8

INGREDIENTS:

- 1 tbsp. canola oil
- 1 red onion, diced
- 2 large waxy potatoes, washed and cut into small dices
- 2 medium parsnips, peeled and diced
- 2 celery stalks, cut into dice
- Black pepper to taste
- 1 tsp fresh, finely chopped basil, plus extra sprigs to serve
- ½ tsp fresh finely chopped oregano

- 1 bay leaf
- 5 cups low sodium fish stock
- 2 cups water
- 2 14.5-ounce cans chopped tomatoes
- 16 ounces grouper filets, skin removed, cut into pieces
- Finely chopped parsley to garnish

DIRECTIONS:

1. In a large pot, heat the oil, then add in the onion, potatoes, parsnips, celery, and black pepper. Fry until the onions are translucent, about 5 minutes.

2. Add in the basil and oregano and stir for 1 minute. Then pour in the stock and water and add the bay leaf.

3. Bring to a steady boil and cook for 15 minutes, or until the potatoes are soft. Add in the tomatoes, and cook, uncovered, for a further 10 minutes to combine the flavors.

4. Lastly, add in the fish pieces and cook until white and flaky, about 3 minutes.

5. Remove the bay leaf and discard.

6. Serve hot, with a sprinkling of parsley to garnish.

Per Serving: 143 calories; 17g carbs; 14g protein; 2g fiber; 714mg sodium; 96mg cholesterol; 2g fat.

FRUITY CHICKEN CURRY

PREP TIME: 5 MINS | COOK TIME: 20 MINS | SERVES: 4

INGREDIENTS:

- 20 ounces chicken breasts, skin removed, and cut into 4 pieces
- 2 tbsp. olive oil, plus extra in a spray bottle
- 1 medium white onion, diced
- 2 Crips apples, peeled, cored, and diced
- 2 small carrots, diced
- 1 tbsp. light curry powder
- ½ cup water
- ¾ cup coconut milk
- 2 tbsp. lemon juice
- ½ cup toasted cashews, to serve

DIRECTIONS:

1. First, brown the meat by oiling a medium pot and frying off the chicken pieces in it. Fry for about 5 minutes in total, until brown and crisp on all sides. Set aside

2. Heat the remaining oil in the same pot and add the onion, apples, and carrots. Fry for 5 minutes before adding in the curry powder and frying for another minute.

3. Pour in the water, coconut milk, and lemon juice, and bring to a slow boil. Then add the chicken pieces back in and cook for about 6 minutes, or until the chicken is cooked through.

4. Serve hot, topped with the cashew nuts.

Per Serving: 444 calories; 26g carbs; 35g protein; 7g fiber; 192mg sodium; 91mg cholesterol; 24g fat.

VEGETARIAN

NORTH-AFRICAN GARBANZO BEAN TAGINE

PREP TIME: 10 MINS | COOK TIME: 45 MINS | SERVES: 2-3

INGREDIENTS:

- ½ cup minced red onion
- 1 cup carrots, diced
- 1 orange flesh sweet potato, cut into small cubes
- 2 tsp olive oil
- ¼ tsp cinnamon
- 2 cinnamon sticks
- ½ tsp cumin
- 1 tsp curry powder
- ½ tsp smoked paprika
- ½ tsp turmeric
- 1 tbsp. tomato paste
- 1 cup low sodium vegetable stock
- 1 ½ cups fresh yellow paprika peppers, diced
- 1 tbsp. minced garlic
- 1 cup cherry tomatoes, diced
- 15 ounces cooked garbanzo beans, rinsed and drained
- ½ cup dates pitted and finely chopped

DIRECTIONS:

1. To start, fry the onion, carrots, and sweet potato in the olive oil, in a medium pot, for about 4 minutes.

2. Then add the cinnamon sticks, cinnamon, cumin, curry powder, smoked paprika, and turmeric. Fry for 1 minute, then add in the tomato paste. Fry for a further minute, and pour in the veg stock. Bring to a low simmer.

3. Add in the fresh paprika, garlic, and tomatoes and cook for 5 minutes.

4. Add the garbanzo beans and dates and simmer, covered for about 30 minutes. The vegetable should all be cooked through and the tagine lovely and aromatic.

5. Serve hot and enjoy.

Quick tips: Traditionally, this dish is made in a Tagine, a Moroccan clay pot. However, a regular pot or casserole dish with a lid works just fine too. Store this is in the fridge for up to 3 days.

Per Serving: 469 calories; 88g carbs; 16g protein; 20g fiber; 256mg sodium; 0mg cholesterol; 9g fat.

CHEESY PASTA BAKE

PREP TIME: 10 MINS | COOK TIME: 35 MINS | SERVES: 8

INGREDIENTS:

- 1 ¼ cups pasta screws
- 1 head Romanesco cauliflower, cut into florets
- 2 tbsp. unsalted butter
- 1 tbsp. corn flour
- 2 cups low fat milk
- 1 tsp hot English mustard
- Olive oil in a spray bottle

- 1 cup grated Gouda cheese
- 1 cup grated Emmental cheese
- Black pepper to taste
- ¼ cup coarsely ground almonds
- ½ tsp ground paprika

DIRECTIONS:

1. Bring a pot of water to a boil and cook the pasta for about 7 minutes.

2. At the same time, bring a smaller pot of water to a boil, and cook the cauliflower florets for about 5 minutes.

3. Drain both the pasta and cauliflower and set aside.

4. Preheat the oven to 350°F.

5. Next, make the sauce. Melt the butter in a medium pot, then whisk in the corn flour, being sure to remove any lumps that form. Gradually add in the milk, whisking all the time to prevent lumps forming. Lastly, mix in the mustard and let the sauce come to a boil.

6. Then add the grated Gouda and Emmental, whisk until they melt, and remove from the heat.

7. Add the pasta and cauliflower into the saucepot and stir well. Add black pepper to taste.

8. Pour the pasta mixture into an oiled casserole dish, and top with the ground almonds. Sprinkle over some paprika and bake in the oven for about 20 minutes until the sauce starts to bubble on the sides.

9. Rest the dish for 5 minutes, then serve hot.

Quick tips: You can swop out the ground almonds for Panko breadcrumbs and the cheeses for any cheese you like. This dish is also great using elbow macaroni instead of pasta screws.

Per Serving: 234 calories; 23g carbs; 13g protein; 2g fiber; 88mg sodium; 30mg cholesterol; 10g fat.

SWEET AND SPICY LENTIL BUNS

PREP TIME: 15 MINS | COOK TIME: 20 MINS | SERVES: 4

INGREDIENTS:

- ¼ cup dried apricots, chopped
- 2 tbsp. tomato paste
- ½ tsp wholegrain mustard
- 1 cup brown lentils, rinsed
- ½ tbsp. coconut oil
- ½ red onion, finely chopped
- 1 green pepper, finely chopped
- ½ cup grated butternut
- 1 stalk celery, finely chopped
- 3 tbsp. finely chopped garlic
- 1 tsp jeera powder
- 2 tsp chili flakes
- 1 tsp smoked paprika
- 15 ounces Marinara sauce
- 1 tbsp. low sodium soy sauce
- 1 tbsp. red wine vinegar
- 4 Soft floury Portuguese bread rolls

DIRECTIONS:

1. In a high powdered blender, blend the apricots, tomato paste, and mustard until they form a smooth paste. Set aside.

2. Bring a small pot of 2 cups of water to a boil, add the lentils and cook for about 20-25 minutes. Drain and set aside.

3. Melt the coconut oil in a medium pot, then add the onion, green pepper, butternut, celery, and garlic and fry for about 5 minutes. Add in the dried spices and fry for a further minute.

4. Then pour in the marinara sauce, soy sauce, red wine vinegar, and apricot paste mixture and cook for 2 minutes.

5. Add in the lentils and bring to a low simmer; cook for 5-10 minutes.

6. Cut the rolls in half and spoon the mixture onto one half. Place the bun tops on the lentils and serve hot.

Quick tips: Serve the lentils on a bed of crunchy lettuce for a lower carb intake.

Per Serving: 269 calories; 50g carbs; 15g protein; 17g fiber; 559mg sodium; 0mg cholesterol; 3g fat.

CHINESE-STYLE STIR-FRIED TOFU

PREP TIME: 10 MINS | COOK TIME: 15 MINS | SERVES: 4

INGREDIENTS:

- 2 tsp rice vinegar
- 2 tbsp. low sodium tomato sauce
- 1 tsp golden syrup
- 2 tsp low sodium soy sauce
- 1 tsp sesame oil
- 1 tbsp. fresh minced chili
- 12 ounces firm tofu, cut into cubes and drained
- 1 tbsp. corn flour
- 2 tbsp. peanut oil

- 4 ounces oyster mushrooms, sliced
- 2 spring onions, sliced
- 2 tbsp. finely chopped garlic
- 4 ounces carrots, cut julienne style
- 2 ounces bamboo shoots, sliced
- 1 ounce celery, cut into large slices
- 1 ounce green beans, cut in half
- 1 ounce bean sprouts

DIRECTIONS:

1. Combine the vinegar, tomato sauce, syrup, soy sauce, sesame oil, and chili in a bowl. Mix well and set aside.

2. Pat off any excess moisture on the tofu until very dry, and coat in the corn flour.

3. Heat 1 tbsp. of the peanut oil in a wok pan, then fry the mushrooms, onions, garlic, carrots, bamboo shoots, green beans, and bean sprouts for about 2-3 minutes.

4. Remove vegetables from the pan, then add the last tbsp. peanut oil. Fry the tofu in the hot oil until all its sides are crisp and brown, about 3 minutes.

5. Pour in the sauce, bring to a boil, and immediately add the vegetables again and cook until heated through.

6. Serve hot and enjoy.

Per Serving: 175 calories; 14g carbs; 9g protein; 2g fiber; 352mg sodium; 0mg cholesterol; 10g fat.

BLACK BEAN MUSHROOM BURGERS

PREP TIME: 15 MINS | COOK TIME: 20 MINS | SERVE: 4

INGREDIENTS:

- 2 tbsp. olive oil
- ½ cup finely chopped brown mushrooms
- ¼ cup finely chopped red onion
- 1 tsp ground cumin
- Black pepper to taste
- 1 tsp barbeque spice
- 1 tsp smoked paprika
- ½ tsp finely chopped fresh thyme
- ½ tsp finely chopped fresh parsley
- 15 ounces black beans, cooked and drained
- ½ cup rolled oats
- 4 burger buns

DIRECTIONS:

1. Heat 1 tbsp. olive oil in a pan, add in the mushrooms and onion and fry until the mushrooms have released all their juices and the onion is translucent for about 4 minutes.

2. Add in the cumin, pepper, barbeque spice, paprika, and fresh herbs, and fry for 1 minute. Then add the black beans and cook for 3 minutes.

3. Remove from the heat, let cool slightly, and mix in the oats. Mix to form a firm burger mixture. Shape 4 burgers from this mixture. Let rest in the fridge for 5 minutes.

4. Heat the remaining oil in a clean pan, and then fry the burger patties for about 4-5 minutes per side, or until a crisp outer layer forms.

5. Serve hot with the buns.

Quick tips: Assemble this burger with all your favorite toppings to serve; lettuce, tomato, mustard mayo, pickles, cheese etc, anything you like will taste good with these delicious burgers. You can freeze these burger patties for up to 3 months.

Per Serving: 368 calories; 66g carbs; 13g protein; 8g fiber; 322mg sodium; 0mg cholesterol; 6g fat.

VEGETARIAN MOROCCAN SPREAD

PREP TIME: 10 MINS | COOK TIME: 65 MINS | SERVES: 6

INGREDIENTS:

Bulgur Wheat:
- ½ cup bulgur wheat
- 1 cup low sodium vegetable stock
- 15 ounces cooked chickpeas, drained

Vegetables:
- 30 ounces pumpkin, peeled and cubed
- 4 large parsnips, sliced thickly
- 2 large baby marrows, cut into thick slices
- 1 large sweet red pepper, cut into large cubes
- 1 red onion, cut into six pieces

- 2 tbsp. olive oil, plus extra in a spray bottle
- 2 tbsp. coarsely chopped garlic
- 1 tsp smoked paprika
- 1 tsp ground ginger
- ½ tsp ground cinnamon
- 1 tsp ground coriander
- Black pepper to taste
- ¼ tsp chili flakes
- 1 cup marinara sauce
- ½ cup water
- Chopped fresh mint to garnish
- 2 lemons, cut into wedges

DIRECTIONS:

1. Preheat the oven to 400°F.

2. In a small pot, bring the veg stock to a boil. Add in the bulgur wheat and chickpeas and turn off the heat. Cover, and let rest until all the liquid is absorbed. Set aside, covered to keep warm.

3. Place all the prepared vegetables in a bowl, add the olive oil and all the ground spices. Mix well, making sure to coat all the vegetables equally in oil and spices.

4. Place on an oiled oven tray and bake in the oven for about 1 hour, or until the vegetables are cooked and lightly browned.

5. Once the vegetables are cooked, place them in a casserole dish, covered to keep warm.

6. Deglaze the roasting tray by placing it over medium heat and adding in the water. Use a wooden spoon to scrape up all the pieces of veg stuck to the tray. Then add in the marinara sauce and bring to a low boil. Pour this mixture over the vegetables and stir well.

7. Just before serving, aerate the bulgur wheat with a fork.

8. To serve, spoon the hot vegetable mixture over the bulgur wheat and garnish with chopped mint and lemon wedges.

Per Serving: 295 calories; 56g carbs; 10g protein; 12g fiber; 431mg sodium; 0mg cholesterol; 6g fat.

NUTTY STUFFED MUSHROOMS

PREP TIME: 20 MINS | COOK TIME: 30 MINS | SERVES: 2

INGREDIENTS:

- ¼ cup unsalted pistachio nuts
- ¼ cup pecan halves
- ¼ cup brown lentils, rinsed
- 4 portobello mushrooms
- 2 tbsp. chipotle chilies in adobo, chopped
- 2 cups riced cauliflower
- 1 tsp cayenne pepper

- 1 tsp jeera powder
- 1 tsp finely chopped garlic
- 1 tsp finely chopped thyme
- 1 tsp ground coriander
- 1 tsp smoked paprika
- 1 lime, juiced
- Olive oil in a spray bottle

DIRECTIONS:

1. Preheat the oven to 375°F.

2. Toast the nuts in a pan over medium heat until golden. Set aside to cool.

3. Bring a small pot of water to a boil, add the lentils, and then cook until soft, about 20 minutes. Drain, rinse under cold water and set aside to cool.

4. Remove the stems and gills from the mushrooms and then place them in a blender with the nuts, chipotle chilies, and lentils. Blitz for about 2 minutes. Do not over blend; some texture is needed.

5. In a separate bowl, mix the cauliflower with the dried spices, fresh herbs, and garlic. Add the lentil mixture to the bowl and mix well.

6. Transfer this mixture onto an oiled oven tray and sprinkle over the lime juice. Bake in the oven for about 15 minutes. Stir once to crisp the underside of the mixture.

7. Place the mushrooms on the same tray, in-between the lentil mixture. Spray the mushrooms with olive oil, and then bake the mushrooms and lentil mixture for a further 20 minutes.

8. To serve, place the mushrooms on a plate and spoon over the crunchy lentil mixture generously.

Per Serving: 364 calories; 33g carbs; 19g protein; 15g fiber; 141mg sodium; omg cholesterol; 19g fat.

CHILI STUFFED BAKED POTATOES

PREP TIME: 10 MINS | COOK TIME: 45 MINS | SERVES: 2

INGREDIENTS:

- 2 large roasting potatoes
- 1 avocado, peeled, cored, and cut into pieces
- ½ a lime, juiced
- Black pepper to taste
- ½ cup red kidney beans, drained and rinsed
- ½ cup homemade spicy tomato salsa
- ½ cup low-fat sour cream
- ¼ tsp Mexican spice blend
- ¼ cup grated gouda cheese
- 2 tsp finely chopped coriander to garnish

DIRECTIONS:

1. Preheat the oven to 400°F. Prick the potatoes with a fork and place them on the oven rack. Bake for 45 minutes until cooked all the way through.

2. In the meantime, prepare the toppings. Smash the avocado and lime juice together in a small bowl and set aside.

3. Mix sour cream and Mexican spice and then mix the beans and salsa in a separate bowl.

4. Once the potatoes are cooked, cut them down the middle and stuff the bean mixture into them. Spoon the avocado onto them and top with sour cream mixture and grated cheese.

5. Serve hot, garnished with coriander, and enjoy.

Per Serving: 624 calories; 91g carbs; 24g protein; 21g fiber; 366mg sodium; 0mg cholesterol; 21g fat.

NUTTY AVOCADO PESTO PASTA

PREP TIME: 10 MINS | COOK TIME: 8 MINS | SERVES: 4

INGREDIENTS:

- 8 ounces chickpea pasta
- 2 cups fresh rocket, tightly packed
- ¼ cup fresh parsley
- ¼ cup roughly chopped almonds
- ²/3 cup baby frozen peas, thawed
- 1 cup fresh basil leaves
- ½ an avocado

- 3 tbsp. garlic, minced
- 2 tbsp. fresh lime juice
- ¼ cup nutritional yeast
- Black pepper to taste
- 3 tbsp. avocado oil
- Fresh basil to garnish

DIRECTIONS:

1. Bring a medium pot of water to a boil and add the chickpea pasta. Cook for about 8 minutes.

2. Next, make your pesto. Using a high-powered blender, blend the rocket, parsley, almonds, peas, basil, avocado, garlic, lime juice, nutritional yeast, and black pepper to taste. Once a paste starts to form, add in the avocado oil and blend until smooth and creamy.

3. Once the pasta is cooked, drain it, and return to the pot. Add in the pesto and stir well to mix evenly.

4. Serve hot, garnished with a sprig of basil.

Quick tips: you can replace the nutritional yeast with parmesan if you like a slightly more traditional flavor.

Per Serving: 417 calories; 43g carbs; 21g protein; 13g fiber; 122mg sodium; 0mg cholesterol; 22g fat.

RISOTTO STYLE BROWN RICE

PREP TIME: 10 MINS | COOK TIME: 75 MINS | SERVES: 2-3

INGREDIENTS:

- 1 cup brown wild rice
- ½ cup diced red onion
- 1 tsp olive oil, plus extra in a spray bottle
- 10 ounces fresh kale
- 1 ½ cups low fat cream cheese
- 1 tbsp. grated pecorino cheese
- ¼ cup coarsely chopped sunflower seeds

DIRECTIONS:

1. Bring a small pot of water to a boil, add the brown wild rice, and cook for about 30 minutes, until soft.

2. Preheat the oven to 375°F.

3. Fry the onion in the olive oil until translucent, about 3minutes. Add the kale, turn off the heat, and cover for 2 minutes to wilt the kale.

4. Once the rice is cooked, drain, and while hot, mix in the cream cheese. Add in the onions and kale and mix well.

5. Lightly oil a deep-bottomed baking dish, and then pour the rice mixture in. Sprinkle the pecorino and sunflower seeds over the top.

6. Bake in the oven for 25 minutes, until the top browns well.

7. Serve hot and enjoy.

Quick tips: Store this dish in the fridge for no more than 3 days and in the freezer for no more than 3 months.

Per Serving: 334 calories; 47g carbs; 19g protein; 5g fiber; 425mg sodium; 0mg cholesterol; 9g fat.

SIDES

ITALIAN ROAST MUSHROOMS

PREP TIME: 5 MINS | COOK TIME: 30 MINS | SERVES: 4

INGREDIENTS:

- 2 tbsp. olive oil
- 10 ounces pink oyster mushrooms
- Black pepper to taste
- 1 tsp fresh basil, chopped
- 1 tsp fresh thyme, finely chopped
- 1 sprig rosemary
- 2 tbsp. garlic, finely sliced

DIRECTIONS:

1. Preheat the oven to 400°F.
2. Oil a baking tray, add all the ingredients except the garlic to the tray. Toss well to coat the mushrooms fully.
3. Roast in the oven for about 25 minutes. Remove from the oven, and layer the garlic beneath the mushrooms, and roast for a further 5 minutes.
4. Serve hot and enjoy.

Per Serving: 94 calories; 5g carbs; 5g protein; 2g fiber; 253mg sodium; 0mg cholesterol; 7g fat.

NUTTY RICED VEGETABLES

PREP TIME: 5 MINS | COOK TIME: 10 MINS | SERVES: 4

INGREDIENTS:

- 2 spring onions, finely chopped
- 3 tbsp. minced fresh garlic
- 1 tbsp. olive oil
- 2 cups riced cauliflower
- 2 cups riced sweet potato
- Black pepper to taste
- 2 tsp fresh thyme, finely chopped

- ¼ cup cashews, roughly chopped
- ¼ cup fresh parsley, chopped

DIRECTIONS:

1. Fry the spring onions and garlic in a medium pan in 1 tbsp. olive oil for about 4 minutes.
2. Add the cauliflower, sweet potato, and black pepper to taste, mix with a wooden spoon, and cook for 5-6 minutes.
3. Turn off the heat and then add in the thyme, cashews, and parsley.
4. Serve warm and enjoy.

Per Serving: 133 calories; 10g carbs; 4g protein; 2g fiber; 50mg sodium; 0mg cholesterol; 10g fat.

CRUNCHY MUSTARD SLAW

PREP TIME: 20 MINS | SERVES: 4

INGREDIENTS:

- 16 ounces green cabbage, cut chiffonade style
- ½ cup walnuts, toasted and roughly chopped
- ½ cup dried cranberries
- ¼ cup olive oil
- 2 tbsp. red wine vinegar
- 2 tsp wholegrain mustard
- Black pepper to taste
- ¼ cup blue cheese, roughly crumbled

DIRECTIONS:

1. Mix the cabbage, walnuts, and cranberries in a bowl. Set aside.
2. Make the dressing by adding the olive oil, red wine vinegar, mustard, and pepper to a small bowl and whisk well to combine.
3. Toss the cabbage mixture and dressing together well.
4. Serve topped with the blue cheese and enjoy.

Quick tips: Swapping the cabbage out for brussels sprouts, cut very finely, is a great alternative to this dish. You can also change the nut variety to any you prefer.

Per Serving: 328 calories; 24g carbs; 7g protein; 6g fiber; 176mg sodium; 6mg cholesterol; 25g fat.

STUFFED SWEET POTATOES

PREP TIME: 5 MINS | COOK TIME: 20 MINS | SERVES: 2

INGREDIENTS:

- ½ cup unsalted pistachios
- Juice of 1 lime
- 2 tsp grated pecorino cheese
- 1 tsp balsamic vinegar
- 2 medium orange flesh sweet potatoes, washed
- 2 tsp olive oil
- 10 ounces broccoli florets

- 2 tsp minced garlic
- 2 tbsp. sun-dried tomatoes, chopped
- Black pepper to taste
- 2 sprigs fresh basil

DIRECTIONS:

1. In a high-powered blender, blitz the pistachios, lime juice, pecorino, and balsamic vinegar, until fine and sticky. Set aside.

2. Prick the sweet potatoes with a fork a few times, then cook them in the microwave for about 7-12 minutes. Time will vary according to the potato sizes. Once cooked, let rest for 5 minutes before cutting lengthways down the center and opening them up.

3. Fry the broccoli florets in the olive oil for about 2 minutes, then add the garlic and fry for another minute. Add the pistachio mixture and the sun-dried tomatoes and cook for another 3 minutes until the tomatoes have softened.

4. Stuff each potato with half of the stuffing mixture, and serve hot, garnished with a sprig of basil.

Per Serving: 409 calories; 52g carbs; 13g protein; 10g fiber; 162mg sodium; 1mg cholesterol; 19g fat.

ITALIAN BEANS AND ENDIVES

PREP TIME: 10 MINS | COOK TIME: 15 MINS | SERVES: 2-3

INGREDIENTS:

- 2 tsp black garlic, minced
- 2 tsp olive oil
- 2 heads Italian endives
- ¼ tsp chili flakes
- 15 ounces cooked white beans, drained
- 1 tbsp. pecorino cheese, shaved

DIRECTIONS:

1. Fry the garlic in the oil in a medium pan for about 2 minutes. Lower the heat and add the endives and fry for about 4 minutes to wilt the greens.

2. Add the chili flakes, add the beans and cook for about 10 minutes until all the flavors are well combined.

3. Serve hot, with a pecorino shaving to top it off.

Per Serving: 225 calories; 34g carbs; 13g protein; 15g fiber; 104mg sodium; 0mg cholesterol; 5g fat.

BUTTERMILK MASH

PREP TIME: 5 MINS | COOK TIME: 28 MINS | SERVES: 6

INGREDIENTS:

- ⅓ cup buttermilk
- 32 ounces mashing potatoes, washed and quartered
- 1 tbsp. coconut oil
- 2 spring onions, finely chopped
- Black pepper to taste

DIRECTIONS:

1. Set the buttermilk in a dish near the stove to warm slightly while cooking the potatoes.

2. Boil the potatoes in a large pot of water for about 25 minutes, until soft and cooked all the way through. Drain them once cooked.

3. Melt the coconut oil in the same pot and then fry the spring onions for about 3 minutes.

4. Add in the potatoes and mash well using a potato masher. Gradually add in the slightly warm buttermilk while mashing. Add black pepper to taste.

5. Serve hot and enjoy.

Per Serving: 136 calories; 27g carbs; 3g protein; 3g fiber; 176mg sodium; 5mg cholesterol; 2g fat.

COCONUT CREAMED CORN

PREP TIME: 5 MINS | COOK TIME: 17 MINS | SERVES: 4

INGREDIENTS:

- 1 tbsp. unsalted butter
- 4 ears sweet corn, shucked and cut off the cob
- 1 cup low fat coconut milk
- 2 tbsp. cake flour
- 1 tsp paprika
- Black pepper to taste

DIRECTIONS:

1. Melt the butter in a medium pot, then add the corn kernels and cook for about 5 minutes, until slightly soft.

2. Whisk the coconut milk and flour together in a small bowl, pour this mixture into the corn pot and stir well. Add in the paprika and pepper and cook for about 12 minutes, stirring regularly.

3. Serve hot and enjoy.

Quick tips: you can swap out the butter for coconut oil and the coconut milk for low fat milk if you like.

Per Serving: 167 calories; 28g carbs; 6g protein; 3g fiber; 189mg sodium; 1mg cholesterol; 5g fat.

GARLICKY CAULIFLOWER MASH

PREP TIME: 10 MINS | COOK TIME: 15 MINS | SERVES: 2-3

INGREDIENTS:

- ½ tsp unsalted butter
- 1 head cauliflower, finely chopped into pieces
- 2 tbsp. garlic, finely chopped
- 3 cups water
- Black pepper to taste
- ¾ cup low fat sour cream

DIRECTIONS:

1. Melt the butter in a medium pan, add in the cauliflower and garlic, and fry 3-4 minutes.

2. Place the cauliflower and garlic in a small pot, cover with water and bring to a boil. Cook for 10 minutes.

3. Drain well and then mash/blend the cauliflower and garlic until smooth. Add black pepper to taste.

4. Pour in the sour cream and mix well.

5. Serve hot and enjoy.

Per Serving: 138 calories; 19g carbs; 15g protein; 6g fiber; 119mg sodium; 0mg cholesterol; 2g fat.

NORTH-AFRICAN BARLEY DISH

PREP TIME: 10 MINS | COOK TIME: 40 MINS | SERVES: 4

INGREDIENTS:

- 1 tbsp. white wine vinegar
- 1 tbsp. honey
- ½ tsp cumin
- ½ tsp cinnamon
- 1 cup barley, rinsed
- 2 ½ cups water
- ¼ tsp pimento pepper
- 2 tbsp. olive oil
- 1 tbsp. minced fresh ginger

- 3 tbsp. thinly sliced fresh garlic
- 4 cups chopped spinach
- ¼ cup sultanas
- ½ cup walnuts, plus extra, chopped to garnish

DIRECTIONS:

1. First, make the dressing by mixing the vinegar, honey, cumin, and cinnamon. Set aside.

2. Add the water to a small pot with the barley and pimento pepper. Bring to a boil and cook for about 30 minutes, until the barley is soft and cooked through.

3. Heat the oil in a frying pan, then add the ginger and garlic and fry for 2 minutes. Add the spinach to the pan and fry for a further 5 minutes.

4. Drain the barley, then mix it with the spinach mixture. Pour the dressing over this, and then stir in the sultanas and walnuts.

5. Serve garnished with the chopped walnuts.

Quick tips: You can swop the barley in this recipe for Farro, a traditional Mediterranean grain.

Per Serving: 422 calories; 57g carbs; 14g protein; 7g fiber; 63mg sodium; 0mg cholesterol; 17g fat.

QUICK VEGGIE RICE

PREP TIME: 5 MINS | COOK TIME: 15 MINS | SERVES: 2-3

INGREDIENTS:

- ½ cup quick-cooking brown rice
- ½ cup chopped zucchini
- ½ cup chopped mushrooms
- 1 cup green beans, cut into pieces
- 1 tsp olive oil
- ¼ cup chopped spring onions
- 1 tsp mild curry powder
- ¼ tsp fresh minced garlic

DIRECTIONS:

1. In a small pot, cook the rice in boiling water for about 5 minutes.

2. Meanwhile, steam the zucchini and beans for about 5 minutes.

3. Heat the oil in a medium pan, add in the mushroom and cook for 2 minutes. Then add the spring onions, curry powder, and garlic and fry for 2 minutes. Add in the steamed veg and cook until all vegetables are cooked through.

4. Drain the rice, then add the vegetable mixture to it, and mix well.

5. Serve hot and enjoy.

Quick tips: you can store this dish in the fridge for up to three days.

Per Serving: 246 calories; 49g carbs; 6g protein; 6g fiber; 51mg sodium; 0mg cholesterol; 4g fat.

DESSERT

BERRY BUTTERMILK PANNA COTTA

PREP TIME: 10 MINS | COOK TIME: 7 MINS | SERVES: 6

INGREDIENTS:

- 2 ¾ cups buttermilk
- 3 tsp plain gelatin powder
- ¼ cup plus 2 tbsp. almond milk
- ½ cup maple syrup
- ½ tsp vanilla essence
- Flavorless oil in a spray bottle
- ½ cup fresh blueberries
- ½ cup fresh strawberries, cut into quarters

DIRECTIONS:

1. Gently warm the buttermilk in a small pot over very low heat. Do NOT boil or overheat, as it will curdle.

2. Then sponge the gelatin by dissolving the gelatin powder in the almond milk in a small glass bowl. Let it sit and absorb for 5 minutes. Place the glass bowl over a pot of very gently simmering water and stir until the gelatin mixture melts completely.

3. Slowly pour the gelatin mixture into the warmed buttermilk and whisk to combine. Then add the maple syrup and vanilla essence and whisk again. Transfer the mixture into a jug and set aside.

4. Lightly oil 6 ramekins and then pour the buttermilk mixture equally into all 6. Place the ramekins on a small tray and cover.

5. Allow the Panna Cottas to set in the fridge for at least 4 hours, but up to 2 days.

6. When ready to serve, very gently loosen the sides of the Panna Cottas with a sharp knife. Run the knife to the bottom to release any air pockets.

7. Turn the ramekins slowly upside-down over the serving plate to gently release the finished product.

8. Garnish equally with the fresh berries and enjoy chilled.

Quick tips: If the Panna Cottas are difficult to remove from their molds, place the bottoms of the ramekins in hot water for about 10 seconds to loosen them further.

Per Serving: 148 calories; 30g carbs; 5g protein; 1g fiber; 127mg sodium; 5mg cholesterol; 1g fat.

ZESTY YOGURT POTS

PREP TIME: 20 MINS | SERVES: 2

INGREDIENTS:

- 2 ounces low fat mascarpone, at room temperature
- ½ cup low fat yogurt
- 2 ½ tbsp. lime juice, plus lime zest to garnish
- 2 tsp honey
- 4 digestive biscuits
- Ready-made whipped cream to serve

DIRECTIONS:

1. Place the mascarpone, yogurt, lime juice, and honey in a bowl and whisk well to combine.

2. In a high-powered blender, blitz the biscuits to a large crumb size, then press these crumbs into the bottoms of two dessert ramekins.

3. Spoon the yogurt mixture into the ramekins, smoothing over the top.

4. Put in the fridge to set for an hour.

5. Serve chilled, topped with whipped cream, and garnished with lime zest.

Quick tips: This dessert lasts well in the fridge for about 2 days.

Per Serving: 219 calories; 18g carbs; 8g protein; 0g fiber; 63mg sodium; 0mg cholesterol; 13g fat.

PEANUT AND CHOCOLATE SQUARES

PREP TIME: 10 MINS | COOK TIME: 30 MINS | SERVES: 9

INGREDIENTS:

- ½ cup dehydrated peanut butter powder
- 2 tbsp. sugar-free smooth peanut butter
- 15 ounces cooked chickpeas, drained
- ¼ cup rolled oats
- ¼ cup unsweetened almond milk
- ¼ cup butternut puree

- ¼ cup stevia
- 2 tsp vanilla essence
- ¾ tsp baking powder
- ⅛ tsp bicarbonate of soda
- Canola oil in a spray bottle
- 2 tbsp. chocolate chips

DIRECTIONS:

1. Preheat the oven to 350°F.

2. Using a high-powered blender, blend the peanut butter powder, peanut butter, chickpeas, oats, almond milk, butternut puree, stevia, vanilla essence, baking powder, and bicarbonate of soda until a thick, smooth batter is formed.

3. Oil an 8 x 8-inch baking dish, and then pour the batter into it.

4. Sprinkle the chocolate chips over the top and press them down lightly.

5. Bake in the oven for about 25 minutes, or until cooked all the way through.

6. Place the tray on a cooling rack and allow it to cool completely before cutting into 9 equal squares.

7. Enjoy.

Quick tips: these squares keep well in a sealed container in the fridge for up to 1 week.

Per Serving: 104 calories; 13g carbs; 6g protein; 4g fiber; 120mg sodium; 0mg cholesterol; 3g fat.

NO-BAKE BERRY TARTS

PREP TIME: 15 MINS | SERVES: 4

INGREDIENTS:

Crust:
- Canola oil in a spray bottle
- 8-10 digestive biscuits
- 2 tsp brown sugar
- 1 tsp melted coconut oil
- ½ cup pecan nuts, finely chopped
- ½ tsp cinnamon

Filling:
- 2 tsp maple syrup
- 1 cup low fat plain yogurt
- ¼ tsp vanilla extract

To serve:
- ½ cup raspberries
- ½ cup blueberries
- 4 sprigs mint
- Ready-made whipped cream

DIRECTIONS:

1. Spray 4 x 4-ounce dessert ramekins with oil to grease. Set aside.
2. Using a blender, blend the digestives, sugar, coconut oil, nuts, and cinnamon until a rough crumb is formed.
3. Line the bottoms and sides of the ramekins with the crumbs, pressing down to ensure it all sticks.
4. Place in the fridge for 2 minutes to set hard.
5. Mix the yogurt, maple syrup, and vanilla and spoon it equally into the set crusts.
6. Garnish with equal amounts of raspberries, blueberries, whipped cream, and top with a sprig of mint.
7. Serve chilled and enjoy.

Per Serving: 211 calories; 21g carbs; 6g protein; 2g fiber; 76mg sodium; 0mg cholesterol; 12g fat.

SIMPLE PEAR CRUMBLE

PREP TIME: 5 MINS | COOK TIME: 35 MINS | SERVES: 6

INGREDIENTS:

- 5 pears, peeled, cored, and cut into large dice
- 2 tbsp. honey
- 1 tbsp. lime juice
- 2 tbsp. corn flour
- ½ tsp cinnamon powder

- Flavorless oil in a spray bottle
- 1 cup homemade Granola

DIRECTIONS:

1. Place the pears, honey, lime juice, corn flour, and cinnamon in a bowl and mix well.

2. Preheat the oven to 350°F.

3. Oil an 11 by 8 ½ inch baking dish lightly, add the pear mixture, bake for 30 minutes, and stir once halfway through the baking.

4. Sprinkle the granola over the top of the pears and return to the oven. Bake for a further 5 minutes. Remove from the oven and allow to rest for 5 minutes.

5. Serve hot and enjoy.

Quick tips: Serving suggestion: serve this with a good dollop of low-fat yogurt over the top.

Per Serving: 201 calories; 38g carbs; 4g protein; 6g fiber; 7mg sodium; 0mg cholesterol; 5g fat.

SPICED FRUITY COOKIES

PREP TIME: 15 MINS | COOK TIME: 10 MINS | SERVES: 12

INGREDIENTS:

- 1 very ripe banana
- ¼ cup smooth almond butter
- 2 tbsp. brown sugar
- 2 tbsp. canola oil, plus extra in a spray bottle
- 1 large egg
- ¼ cup rolled oats
- ½ tsp vanilla essence

- ½ cup cake flour
- ¼ tsp baking powder
- ¼ tsp cinnamon
- ⅛ tsp cloves
- ⅛ tsp nutmeg
- ¼ pecan nuts, roughly chopped

DIRECTIONS:

1. Preheat the oven to 350°F.

2. Place the banana, almond butter, sugar, and oil in a bowl. Mash up the banana and then whisk well to combine the ingredients thoroughly. Then add in the egg, oats, and vanilla essence and mix well.

3. Sift together the dry ingredients: flour, baking powder, cinnamon, cloves, and nutmeg. Add in the nuts and mix.

4. Combine the wet and dry ingredients to form a firm cookie dough.

5. Roll out 12 balls using your hands. Then place them on a well-oiled baking sheet and press down to form cookies.

6. Bake for 8-10 minutes, and remove from the oven to cool.

Quick tips: Store these in a sealed container, once cooled, for up to 5 days. You can also freeze them for 3 months.

Per Serving: 122 calories; 12g carbs; 3g protein; 1g fiber; 8mg sodium; 0mg cholesterol; 7g fat.

CHOCO-FUDGE COOKIES

PREP TIME: 10 MINS | COOK TIME: 15 MINS | SERVES: 12

INGREDIENTS:

- 15 ounces cooked chickpeas, rinsed and drained
- 3 tbsp. smooth pecan nut butter
- ½ cup cocoa powder, unsweetened
- ½ cup rolled oats
- ¼ cup pumpkin puree
- 1 tsp vanilla essence
- 1 tsp cinnamon
- 1 tsp baking powder

- ¼ cup stevia
- 2 tbsp. almond milk
- 6 tbsp. egg whites
- ½ tsp honey
- Canola oil in a spray bottle

DIRECTIONS:

1. Preheat the oven to 350°F

2. Using a high-powered blender, blend all the ingredients to form a firm cookie dough.

3. Lightly grease a baking sheet, then spoon out 12 cookies into the sheet. Press them down slightly and then bake for about 15 minutes, or until firm.

4. Let cool and serve.

Per Serving: 65 calories; 12g carbs; 5g protein; 3g fiber; 78mg sodium; 1mg cholesterol; 1g fat.

PUMPKIN POTS

PREP TIME: 10 MINS | COOK TIME: 35 MINS | SERVES: 4

INGREDIENTS:

- ¼ tsp canola oil, plus extra in a spray bottle
- 2 tbsp. almonds, roughly chopped
- ½ cup almond milk
- 1 cup unsweetened pumpkin puree
- 1 large egg
- 2 tbsp. honey
- ¼ tsp cinnamon
- ¼ tsp nutmeg
- ¼ tsp ground cloves
- ¼ tsp ground ginger

DIRECTIONS:

1. Preheat the oven to 350°F.

2. Heat ¼ tsp oil in a medium pan and fry the nuts for about 2 minutes. Remove from the heat and drain.

3. Mix the almond milk, pumpkin, egg, honey, and ground spices in a large bowl. Stir well to ensure a smooth texture.

4. Lightly grease the insides of 4 ramekins, and then pour the pumpkin mix into the. Sprinkle the nuts over the top.

5. Fill a large deep-bottomed baking dish with a bit of water, then place the ramekins in the dish. Make sure the water doesn't come up to more than a ¼ way up the sides of the ramekins.

6. Bake in the oven for 25-30 minutes, until firm and set.

7. Allow to rest for 5 minutes, serve them warm, and enjoy.

Quick tips: you can store these covered for up to 5 days in the fridge.

Per Serving: 112 calories; 14g carbs; 4g protein; 2g fiber; 35mg sodium; 0mg cholesterol; 5g fat.

COCONUT, STRAWBERRIES AND CHOCOLATE

PREP TIME: 2 MINS | COOK TIME: 4 MINS | SERVES: 4

INGREDIENTS:

- 5 ounces 70% dark chocolate, chopped finely
- ½ cup low fat coconut milk
- ½ tsp orange zest
- 24 strawberries, stalks and leaves still on

DIRECTIONS:

1. Place the chocolate in a medium glass bowl.

2. Heat the coconut milk in a small pot, bringing it almost to a boil. Then add the orange zest and pour it over the chocolate.

3. Let this mixture sit for about 3 minutes, then stir well to mix in the now melted chocolate.

4. Serve the strawberries with a ramekin of the sauce to dip them in.

Per Serving: 229 calories; 28g carbs; 5g protein; 4g fiber; 36mg sodium; 3mg cholesterol; 14g fat.

VERY-BERRY MUG CAKE

PREP TIME: 3 MINS | COOK TIME: 4 MINS | SERVES: 1

INGREDIENTS:

- ¼ tsp canola oil, plus extra in a spray bottle
- 2 tbsp. low fat sour cream
- 2 tbsp. low fat almond milk
- 1 large egg white
- ½ tsp almond extract
- 3 cherries, stoned and diced
- 1 strawberry, diced

- ¼ cup cake flour
- 1 ½ tsp stevia powder
- ¼ tsp baking powder

DIRECTIONS:

1. In a small bowl, mix the ¼ tsp oil, sour cream, almond milk, egg white, almond extract, cherries, and strawberry. Set aside.

2. In another small bowl, mix the flour, stevia, and baking powder.

3. Whisk together the two bowls of ingredients to form a smooth cake batter.

4. Lightly oil a microwave-safe mug, then pour the cake batter into it.

5. Microwave on high for 3-4 minutes, or until cooked.

6. As soon as the mug comes out of the microwave, run a knife around the edges to loosen the cake. Flip upside-down over a serving plate and remove from the mug.

7. Allow to cool before serving.

Per Serving: 180 calories; 30g carbs; 11g protein; 5g fiber; 237mg sodium; 2mg cholesterol; 2g fat.

MOIST CHOCOLATE BROWNIES

PREP TIME: 15 MINS | COOK TIME: 30 MINS | SERVES: 9

INGREDIENTS:

- 2 large eggs
- ½ cup cocoa powder
- ⅔ cup caster sugar
- 14 ounces cooked black beans, rinsed and drained
- 3 tbsp. olive oil
- ½ tsp baking powder
- ½ cup chocolate chips
- 2 tbsp. pecan nut pieces
- Canola oil in a spray bottle

DIRECTIONS:

1. Preheat the oven to 350°F.

2. Place all the ingredients, except for ¼ cup chocolate chips and the pecan nuts, in a high-powered blender, and blend on high to form a smooth batter.

3. Lightly oil an 8 by 8-inch baking tin, and pour the brownie mixture into it. Scatter the remaining chocolate chips and pecan nuts over the top.

4. Bake in the oven for about 30 minutes, or until just cooked.

5. Allow to cool before cutting into 9 equal brownies and serving.

Quick tips: These brownies can be stored, sealed in the fridge for 3 days, and in the freezer for 30 days.

Per Serving: 214 calories; 32g carbs; 5g protein; 5g fiber; 23mg sodium; 0mg cholesterol; 9g fat.

METRIC EQUIVALENCE CHART

Volume Measurements		Weight Measurements		Temperature Conversion	
U.S.	Metric	U.S.	Metric	Fahrenheit	Celsius
1 teaspoon	5 ml	1/2 ounce	15 g	250	120
1 tablespoon	15 ml	1 ounce	30 g	300	150
1/4 cup	60 ml	3 ounces	85 g	325	160
1/3 cup	80 ml	4 ounces	115 g	350	175
1/2 cup	125 ml	8 ounces	225 g	375	190
2/3 cup	160 ml	12 ounces	340 g	400	200
3/4 cup	180 ml	1 pound	450 g	425	220
1 cup	250 ml	2-1/4 pounds	1 kg	450	230

Made in the USA
Las Vegas, NV
16 October 2021